MW01006205

Praise for *Humbitious*

"This book makes a compelling case that you don't need a big ego to do great things. Amer Kaissi demonstrates that humility isn't a sign of weakness—it's a source of strength for leaders."

ADAM GRANT #1 *New York Times* bestselling author of *Think Again* and host of the TED podcast *WorkLife*

"How can leaders display humility while remaining ambitious? Amer Kaissi reveals the fascinating answers in this entertaining and evidence-based book."

DR. TASHA EURICH organizational psychologist and *New York Times* bestselling author of *Insight* and *Bankable Leadership*.

"Too often, we underestimate the enormous strength it takes to practice skills like kindness and humility. With *Humbitious*, Amer Kaissi has exposed humility not just as a virtue worth striving for, but also as a valuable tool for success. I highly recommend this book for readers at any stage of their leadership journey."

DANIEL LUBETZKY founder of KIND Snacks

"An entertaining and brilliantly compelling argument for humble honesty. In an era when brash celebrity is often marketed as leadership, Amer Kaissi deftly weaves research and the experiences of leaders—some impressive and some not—into a convincing case that humility unlocks our potential."

GEN. STANLEY MCCHRYSTAL U.S. Army (Ret.), Joint Special Operations Command

"In a world where leadership models are changing, Amer Kaissi's book clarifies the notion that effective leaders succeed the most when they relate and connect to the people around them. Kaissi shatters the myths about what humility really means, and shows us that it is not weakness, but actually requires inner confidence and a strength of character many don't possess. He demonstrates that arrogance and dictatorship may help in the very short term, but rarely lead to sustainable, impactful success. Read this book to ask yourself the tough questions and get inspired to adopt a new model of leadership success."

MARIA ROSS brand strategist, speaker, and author of *The Empathy Edge*

"In masterful fashion, Kaissi brings humility to life. Through inspiring stories and clear summaries of academic research, *Humbitious* illuminates why humility is a vital strength for anyone wanting to make a positive impact. A must-read for anyone who wants to elevate their leadership potential and effectiveness."

DR. BRAD OWENS associate professor, Marriott School of Management, Brigham Young University, and one of the world's foremost experts on humble leadership

"For those who often hear the buzzword 'humility' but wonder what it really means and whether it works, Amer Kaissi's *Humbitious* is a must-read. Not just another person's opinion or preaching of humility, his book is based on decades of cumulative scientific evidence on the effectiveness of humility in improving individual performance and relationships with others, and in transforming teams and organizations."

DR. AMY OU associate professor, humility researcher, Department of Management and Marketing, The Hong Kong Polytechnic University

Humbitious

Humbitious

The Power of Low-Ego, High-Drive Leadership

AMER KAISSI

PAGE TWO

Cataloguing in publication information is available from
Library and Archives Canada.

978-1-77458-073-8 (paperback)
978-1-77458-074-5 (ebook)

Page Two
pagetwo.com

Edited by James Harbeck
Copyedited by Melissa Edwards
Cover design by Jennifer Lum and Setareh Ashrafologhalai
Interior design by Setareh Ashrafologhalai
Interior illustrations by Setareh Ashrafologhalai
Printed in Canada

21 22 23 24 25   5 4 3 2 1

amerkaissi.com

Dedicated to my wife, Wafaa, and
children, Maria and Adam
To my parents, Nahida and Anis
And especially to my late grandmother,
Durriya (Teta Imm Anis)

Contents

Foreword

ANIELA WAS a rising star at a capital management firm. Everyone in the company agreed she would be a senior leader one day... *if* she could learn to "play nice with others in the sandbox."

Her 360-degree feedback report was full of phrases like, "Daniela is brilliant but she has sharp elbows," and "She has to get better with people if she wants to advance." I was brought in as her executive coach to help build her people skills.

Daniela knew she was impatient. She told me she had never suffered fools gladly and didn't mind if people read her that way.

During our coaching, she determinedly experimented with new behaviors and new thoughts that strengthened her awareness of her impact on others. More than once she reported back to me that her biggest take-away was this: in order to consider others more often, she would need to think of herself as being "of service." Intellectually she understood that, were she able to consider others more, she would most likely achieve her ambitions sooner. But in practice it was hard.

A quite different leader was Anish.

Anish was a division president for a national homebuilder. His coaching was triggered because people wanted him to move faster. His feedback report was full of phrases like, "He's the most democratic leader I've ever worked for. Great, but please, a little less democracy and a little more action," and "He's got plenty of good will in the bank. He should trade on that and get stuff done."

He was grateful for the coaching. He had foreseen that, to be successful as a president, he would need to gain mastery over his reliance on humility and gain more skills in achievement. This was not completely new in his life. He told me his friends and family joked that he was like "Minnesota nice" on steroids.

During his coaching, Anish found he was actually quite good at getting stuff done. When exerting that part of himself, he found that it didn't cause conflict; rather, people were appreciative. They liked him as much as ever. He began to inhabit the role of president in a way that felt integrated and authentic.

It has now been more than a decade since I coached Daniela and Anish. I've stayed in contact with them and have watched their stories evolve. They're both quite happy.

Anish continued his success as a division president. He learned to draw as often on his reservoir of achievement skills as he did on his natural humility. Then new owners took over. He discovered, sadly, that the new owners did not value humility. In less than a year, Anish left the company and found a new position where he was happier.

Daniela built team after team at her company. All delivered high performance. Her teams swelled into a department, then into a division. To this day, that division is hers to run. Go to the company's website and you'll see her pictured as one of the senior leaders. She loves her career.

Daniela is often invited to speak on panels. She talks openly about herself, admitting she'd never have achieved her goals if she hadn't toned down her ambition and learned some humility. Remembering the woman who "didn't suffer fools gladly," she laughs, saying, "Now I'm just one of the fools!"

She and Anish consciously chose to develop and balance two facets of themselves that are within us all: humility and ambition. The balance has made them each stand out. They both have devoted followers.

When I first read *Humbitious,* I was struck by two thoughts.

First, I thought of Daniela and Anish. I wished I'd had the book when I was coaching them. Amer shares compelling research, making a clear case that leaders who are able to balance humility and ambition achieve higher results. Had Daniela and Anish been able to read *Humbitious,* it would've accelerated their paths to success.

Second, I thought of you, the current and rising leaders who search for your own balance between humility and ambition. Amer's stories and research will awaken a path in you that will guide you towards self-awareness, open-mindedness, and appreciation. Without the first, leaders cannot experience growth. Without the second, they cannot gain wisdom. Without the third, they cannot generate devotion. *Humbitious* will help you develop all three.

This is a path of many riches. Enjoy the journey.

TOM HENSCHEL

TOM HENSCHEL is one of America's leading executive coaches. He runs the development firm Essential Communications. For more than a decade he has hosted *The Look & Sound of Leadership* podcast, rated in the top 1 percent of all 2 million podcasts globally.

Introduction

THIS BOOK IS for leaders at all stages who want to improve their performance and who are struggling with their ego but may not realize that both humility and ambition are vital for effective leadership. By the time you finish reading this book, I hope, you will have changed your mindset about humility and learned new behaviors and habits for high-performing leadership.

One of the most common myths about leadership is that arrogant, overconfident, and even narcissistic individuals are better leaders. Let me shatter this myth right off the bat: tons of research that I will share throughout this book unequivocally shows that such leaders are not effective or successful over time. It's very clear: self-centered leaders do not achieve success in the long term. "But our current CEO is an arrogant jerk!" you might say. Yes, arrogant jerks are often chosen for leadership positions, but the evidence is very clear that they are not effective in the long term, because they tend to be cold, hostile managers and lousy team players. The successful narcissists that you either know or are working for right now are the exception to the rule. It is humility that leads to higher performance.

I have dedicated the last eight years of my career studying, understanding, coaching, and speaking about humility with thousands of people across the world. But humility has been part of my development since my childhood in Lebanon, a small country in the Middle East. I was born exactly one year after the Lebanese Civil War erupted. While growing up in a violent war that killed thousands and displaced millions is significant enough in and of itself, the most influential experience of my childhood was actually going to work with my mother every day. She was the director for one of the largest faith-based orphanages in the country, and she worked every day till late in the evening, including Saturdays and holidays. Every day after school, on weekends, and especially during summer breaks, I would go with her to work. She would drop me off in the playground, and I would spend the whole time with the children who lived in the orphanage. I played with them, ate with them, and learned to see the world through their eyes.

While my family was middle class, I spent the majority of my childhood playing with kids who didn't have much, who had lost one or both of their parents in the war, or whose parents had given them up because they were too poor to take care of them. When my eighth birthday approached, my parents offered to invite my classmates from school to the party. But I insisted that I wanted my friends from the orphanage to celebrate my birthday with me. Two dozen orphaned children came to our house to eat cake and play games; for most, this was their first time ever attending a real birthday party outside of the orphanage. These experiences molded me and taught me important lessons about humility. I learned to appreciate the privileges into which I was born and to build relationships and friendships with everyone, regardless of their social or economic status.

Years later, after finishing college in Lebanon, I was fortunate enough to come to the United States to do my graduate studies, which presented me with different lessons in humility. As a twenty-three-year-old, I did one of the worst things you can do at that age: I started a PhD in the doctoral program in health services administration at the University of Minnesota. I was, by far, the youngest student; most others were in their thirties, forties, fifties. They called me the "baby of the class." They brought with them extensive experience, while I had never held a full-time job. They discussed previous work situations and told stories about their colleagues and bosses. I barely opened my mouth. I mostly listened and took notes. This significant experience taught me the importance of knowing my limits, acknowledging my ignorance, and learning from others.

Having said that, I believe that I still have a long way to go to reach personal humility. While I have been fortunate to experience situations that taught me some valuable lessons, my natural tendencies are to show off, seek attention, and talk more than I listen. In that sense, I can relate to Benjamin Franklin, who, after working hard on practicing various virtues in his day-to-day behaviors, finally admitted that humility was the hardest one to conquer because it went against his nature. That's why this book is for me as much as it is for other people. As Franz Kafka once observed, "A book must be the axe for the frozen sea within us." I hope that, by writing this book, I can make further progress on my own journey to gain more humility.

In 2003, I took my first full-time faculty position at Trinity University in San Antonio. As I began teaching graduate students, I wondered whether the lessons I had learned about humility were related to the effectiveness of leaders working in hospitals and other healthcare organizations. The more

I thought about this, the more I realized that our educational system and organizational hiring practices are set up to penalize humble people and reward self-promoting egocentrics. I sifted through the research and discovered the negative impact of not recognizing and rewarding humility; the evidence clearly showed that humble leaders outperform non-humble ones in all long-term measures. In 2017, I wrote *Intangibles: The Unexpected Traits of High-Performing Healthcare Leaders* to uncover—based on research—the traits necessary for high performance in healthcare. I found that humility, compassion, kindness, and generosity, when combined with ambition, competence, strength, and accountability, enable leaders to achieve high performance for themselves, their teams, and their organizations.

After that book was published, I got invited to give talks to groups and organizations all over the world. At these events, leaders from all levels showed great interest in the concept of humility. Based on what I heard in these talks and in professional social media platforms, I realized that humility is not just a crucial trait for healthcare leaders, it is also paramount for all types of leaders in all industries. So, in this book, I want to share with you what I have learned about humility based on my experiences and on the scientific research that has been published in the last fifteen years.

The main idea in this book is that humility, when combined with ambition, can significantly improve your performance and the performance of your teams and organization. Since the beginning of humanity, no major achievement has ever been accomplished by one person; humans have always needed to collaborate and help each other, and for that they need to be humble enough to recognize their own limitations and ask for that help. This is even truer now, as the world is becoming more unknowable and unpredictable. New technology, hand-held devices, and accessible platforms pump out new facts and opinions by the second. In the face of this information deluge, humans are predictably irrational and biased. Our decisions are based on emotional reactions and heuristic shortcuts rather than on logical analysis, which is especially inadequate in the age of mega-information. You can't know everything or do anything by yourself. You need to rely on others for help, ideas, and advice. And for that, you need to be humble.

Moreover, there is an "illusion of knowledge" in our society, especially among leaders. They rarely acknowledge gaps in their knowledge, and they believe they know more than they actually do. The historian Yuval Noah Harari recently noted that "some people who know next to nothing about meteorology or biology nevertheless propose policies regarding climate change and genetically modified crops, while others hold extremely strong views about what should be done in Iraq or Ukraine without being able to locate these countries on a map." And while narcissism is commonplace in the current political and social climate, a large portion of the population, especially younger people, are turned off by egotistical leaders and would much rather vote for and work for leaders who display empathy and humility.

While humility has always been important, it will be a vital survival skill in the near future. With the rise of artificial intelligence, robots and smart machines are expected to replace human beings in more than half of the current jobs in the economy. The only human skills that will be needed in the new world are team-based ones that machines cannot yet replicate, such as critical contemplation, innovative thinking, and emotional engagement with others. Edward Hess from the University of Virginia notes that the common thread running through these distinctly human skills is humility.

Given all these factors, there is an urgent need for a book on humility in leadership that is both research-based and accessible to a large number of people. Most books on the topic either rely on opinion and personal experience or are too theoretical and out of touch with the world of practice. I believe that the concept of humble leadership has not yet caught on because the prevalent advice and models are not based on evidence. I felt the need to write a book that doesn't just give the generic advice to "be more humble," but also summarizes the data and findings in order to suggest specific evidence-based practices. As W. Edwards Deming once said, "Without data, you're just another person with an opinion."

And there is data. There has been a remarkable explosion in the research on humility in the last few years. The problem is that most of that research is in articles published in inaccessible academic journals. I have sifted through this research and translated it into everyday English, combining it with interesting stories and case studies so that it can be put into practice by all leaders in all organizations. Many of the leaders I interact with in my coaching, speaking, and teaching engagements ask me, "What are the most effective humble behaviors? What are potential pitfalls of being a humble leader? It is possible to learn how to be humble?" I wrote this book to answer these questions. I've curated, evaluated, and synthesized all the research published on humility in scientific journals in order to help you make sense of it and put it to use in the right way. To reduce disruptions while you're reading, I didn't include references in the text, but you can access the studies and resources for each chapter in the Notes at the end of the book.

An important goal of this book is to help you understand, based on evidence, what humility is and is not. This may seem like a simple question, but there is a common lack of understanding about what true humility is. Humility is not weakness, lack of self-esteem, or low assertiveness. In fact, it is the exact opposite, since it requires strength, courage, and fierce determination. Humility is about having a true understanding of your strengths and weaknesses. If you believe you are good at something based on your expertise and say, "I am good at this, but I am not the only one who is good at it," you are not being arrogant; you are actually confidently humble. Disparaging yourself in public and saying, "I'm not that good" while secretly believing that you are better than everyone else is false humility.

Humility, as you will see in the course of this book, has many aspects. It involves knowing your strengths and weaknesses and reflecting on them, being vulnerable, being open-minded and teachable, being grateful towards others, and acknowledging that you are an infinitely small part of the universe. I believe that there is nothing more important for you as a leader to practice and model than humility and ambition.

one

An Overview of Humility and Ambition in Leadership

— 1 —

What Is Humble Leadership?

Humility is the foundation of all the other virtues: hence,
in the soul in which this virtue does not exist there
cannot be any other virtue except in mere appearance.

ST. AUGUSTINE

"Jacinda-mania"

Jacinda Ardern was born in Dinsdale, a small working-class town of 8,000 people. Her father was a police officer and her mother worked in the school cafeteria. To help make ends meet, the family owned a little side business selling apples and pears, and little Jacinda would help on the tractor every day after school. One day at school, she noticed that some girls were unhappy because of mean comments made by other students, so she started a "Happy Club" and instructed members that they could say only nice things. When she was sixteen, she took another job as a cashier at the local grocery store, and when a customer was short on money, Jacinda dipped into her own wallet and paid the difference.

In high school, Jacinda got involved in the student council, the debate team, and the human rights group, and worked for the school newspaper. She organized her fellow classmates to fight the school's policy of banning female students from wearing pants, and never took no for an answer. Once, she was assigned a research paper on a famous legislator, Marilyn Waring, but she couldn't find many written resources on her. What did Jacinda do? She called Waring personally and got the information she needed!

Soon after, she was off to college at the University of Waikato, a school known for its diverse student body, where she studied politics and public relations. Her professors could already see her personality and potential: "We teach students, but there are some students we learn from as well, and I would say that she was one of those students," noted Debashish Munshi, one of Jacinda's communication professors. The faculty described her as a humble, socially conscious, and talented communicator.

After graduation, it wasn't long before she got involved in politics. She worked as a researcher in the prime minister's office and got elected as president of the International Union of Socialist Youth. And then, at the young age of twenty-eight, she became a member of Parliament representing the Labor Party. While she was already well known in her country, the world didn't take notice of Jacinda Ardern until October 26, 2017, when she became New Zealand's prime minister. "Jacinda-mania" was unleashed.

What makes Jacinda Ardern so unique as a leader is how unassuming and humble she is. When a couple of *Time* correspondents went to interview her shortly after the election, she was genuinely taken aback when they told her that she was the youngest female leader in the world. Her home after the

election remained the same modest three-bedroom bunga-
low that she shared with her partner and that they renovated
and painted themselves.

So often, when a humble leader emerges in business or in
politics, cynics are quick to note that the "soft stuff" is all nice
and good, but they question whether that leader has what it
takes to get results. Do they have the required steel to address
tough situations and deal with difficult people? Not surprisingly, the same questions were asked of Jacinda Ardern. Bryce
Edwards, New Zealand's leading political commentator,
noted, "Many people, myself included, have struggled to see
how her advocacy of the politics of kindness is anything more
than sloganeering that lacks any real substance." And while
to outsiders New Zealand looks like a pristine country with
green hills and white sheep, many serious challenges were
waiting to test the new leader's strength, such as record levels
of childhood poverty, youth suicide, domestic violence, meth
addiction, and inadequate housing.

And then things got much worse. On Friday, March 15,
2019, in the small town of Christchurch, a terrorist drove to a
mosque and started shooting worshippers while live stream-
ing the attack on Facebook. He then continued the shooting
spree at an Islamic center. In all, he killed fifty-one people
and injured forty-nine others. New Zealand and the world
were shocked. A few hours after the attack, Jacinda Ardern
responded with a tweet that was shared millions of times
around the world: "What has happened in Christchurch is an
extraordinary act of unprecedented violence. It has no place
in New Zealand. Many of those affected will be members
of our migrant communities—New Zealand is their home—
they are us." In those difficult times, she wanted to send a
message of inclusiveness to the victims and their families.

And nothing could have been more inclusive than "they are us."

Over the following few days, Ardern made several appearances in the neighborhoods affected by the shootings. Modestly dressed in a black headscarf out of respect for the Muslim community, she showed genuine grief, empathy, and humility. She hugged people and held their hands. She told them she supported them and asked for their suggestions. The community responded with overwhelming admiration for the young leader. Ahmed Bahmji, the chairperson of one of the mosques Ardern visited, said to her, "We are forever grateful the day that our hearts were broken, you looked straight at us . . . and spoke to us in a way that restored our hearts, restored our faith and restored our community."

But Ardern was careful not the make the tragic occasion about herself: at memorial services, she didn't speak more than she needed to; instead, she allowed the survivors, the victims' families, and local imams to dialogue and grieve. The most-shared image of her during that time period was not of her addressing a large crowd; rather, it was an image of her appearing heartbroken as she looked out a window during a private meeting with mourners. While Jacinda Ardern's humility, compassion, and inclusiveness were praised all around the world, it was her subsequent actions that taught us valuable lessons in leadership.

First, she addressed the terrorist with stern words: "You may have chosen us, but we utterly reject and condemn you." In a speech later in Parliament, she refused to say his name, explaining that she didn't want to give him the notoriety that he most sought. Before long, she went after Facebook and other social medial platforms, asking them to put policies in place to take responsibility for the hateful content posted on their pages. And then, most significantly, she led the country in passing sweeping changes to its gun laws, banning all assault rifles and military-style semi-automatic weapons.

For the citizens of New Zealand, Jacinda Ardern's perfect balance of humility and strength made her an instant hero. A woman who was interviewed at the time captured the nation's collective emotions: "Jacinda has been a beacon of hope in New Zealand's darkest time. She's behaved with such compassion, strength and integrity. I've never felt prouder to be a New Zealander." Even skeptic Bryce Edwards couldn't help but be impressed: "So far, it seems that Ardern has not put a foot wrong in dealing with the crisis. She's been absolutely superb."

The Christchurch attack was a tragic—but perfect—time for the young prime minister to show her approach to leadership. Less than a year later, COVID-19 presented another major test that she and the country passed again with flying colors. Humility and compassion were abundant in her frequent Facebook live chats, where she came across as both authentic and reassuring. During the crisis, the large majority of Kiwis trusted the government to make the right decisions in addressing the crisis. And the government delivered on that trust: at the time of writing, New Zealand had less than 2,500 cases of the novel coronavirus, nearly all of which had recovered. Only twenty-six deaths had been registered in a country of five million people!

The idea that humility and compassion are soft traits that cannot be combined with strength and determination has been shattered by Jacinda Ardern and her leadership style. "One of the criticisms I've faced over the years is that I'm not aggressive enough or assertive enough, or maybe somehow, because I'm empathetic, it means I'm weak. I totally rebel against that. I refuse to believe that you cannot be both compassionate and strong," she noted long before 2019. Ardern illustrates the main idea in this book: leaders who strive to achieve high performance must combine humility with ambition. Ambition is striving to achieve important things not only for oneself but also for the collective: the team, the organization, and even the community and the world. It comprises strength, action, and determination. But we're getting ahead of ourselves. Before we go any further, let's look at what "humility" means.

Humus (Not the Dip)

As long as humans have written about virtues, humility has been included among them. The word "humility" originates from the Latin *humus* (not be confused with the delicious Middle Eastern dip), which means close to the ground or to the earth. Stoic philosophy, for example, viewed humility as desirable because it allowed people to think wisely about their place in the world and urged them to conquer their pride by intentionally lowering themselves. Seneca, the pioneering Stoic philosopher, purposefully experimented with poverty to prevent his wealth from corrupting him, while Marcus Aurelius, the great Roman emperor, constantly reminded himself of his own mortality to prevent power from going to his head.

Similarly, the Eastern religions and philosophies acknowledge humility as necessary for human excellence. But they have taken a slightly different approach in focusing on the ability to let go of the self and connect with a greater reality (which we will refer to as transcendence). For the Buddhists, the path to enlightenment involves awareness of things as they really are and freeing oneself from selfishness through humble thought and action, while the Taoists conceived of humility as losing the self and serving others. The ancient Chinese philosopher Confucius, in his famous *Analects*, described the humble person as one who does not boast and who asks for advice without shame. Followers of the monotheistic Abrahamic religions of Christianity, Islam, and Judaism also believe in humility as submission to and before God.

In Europe, the Age of Enlightenment witnessed similar interpretations of humility. For example, Dutch philosopher Baruch Spinoza pointed out that without humility, the mind lacks adequate knowledge of itself and fails to realize that something greater than itself exists. The German philosopher Immanuel Kant stressed that humility is realizing that you are "a dependent and corrupt but capable and dignified rational agent."

In the last twenty years, the study of humility by philosophers and psychologists have continued to focus on examining the self. Especially noteworthy is the work of French philosopher André Comte-Sponville, who reasoned that humility is the extreme awareness of our limitations that derives from everything that we are not. So he advocated for an accurate assessment of one's strengths and weaknesses. A recent refocus on humility as a positive human trait can be credited to the field of positive psychology, which argues that humility is about taking an accurate look at the self, but without self-disparagement.

The Three Building Blocks

Building on these cultural, religious, and philosophical understandings, let us frame humility in leadership as consisting of three main building blocks:

1   how you understand yourself (self-awareness, self-reflection, and vulnerability);

2   how you understand your relationships with others (open-mindedness, appreciation of others, and generosity); and

3   how you understand your place in the universe (transcendence).

First, you have to start with understanding yourself, and then you understand your relationship with others, which eventually allows you to reach the final step in your journey as a humbitious leader: understanding your place in the universe.

The first block:
How you understand yourself

Humility is first and foremost about having an accurate view of yourself. Although some people—and even some dictionaries—view humility as synonymous with low self-esteem, psychology and leadership experts describe humility as understanding one's talents and accomplishments while accepting one's imperfections and shortcomings. Robert Emmons, professor of psychology at the University of California, Davis, clarifies that "to be humble is not to have a low opinion of oneself, it is to have an accurate opinion of oneself." When you have a talent or special skill and you don't acknowledge it, you are not displaying humility. Rather, you are engaging in self-disparagement and possibly ingratitude. As a humble, smart leader, you should recognize that you are smart but you should also know that you are not smarter than everyone else—or smarter than the collective intelligence of the group that you lead. You can appreciate that you have expertise in strategy, for example, but you should also acknowledge that you don't know everything about the subject and that you still have a lot to learn.

Humility is not about deflating or inflating your abilities or status; it is about understanding them just the way they are. You can strive to know your strengths and weaknesses based on disciplined self-reflection. This is especially challenging when you get promoted to higher positions and are granted great power and authority. Unless you practice humility intentionally, your views of yourself can easily get skewed, especially if you believe everything you are told by some of the sycophants who may have surrounded you.

The second block:
How you understand your relationships with others

Once you are aware of your personal limitations, you can be open to new ideas and ways of thinking, and you become willing to learn from others. The clever organizational theorist Karl Weick perfectly captured this when he encouraged leaders to admit the shortcomings of their knowledge: "When a leader is able to humbly admit 'I don't know,' that admission forces the leader to drop pretense, drop omniscience, drop expert authority, drop a macho posture, and drop monologues... listening and exploring is the consequence."

You then ask for advice, you seek and listen to honest feedback from others, and you even solicit contradictory views. Brad Owens, professor of business ethics at Brigham Young University and one of the leading researchers in the field of humble leadership, describes this quality as "teachability": the willingness to admit ignorance, appreciate others' contributions, and learn from them. Teachability entails having an open mind, a curiosity towards others, and an interest in understanding them and their views.

The third block:
How you understand your place in the universe

One of the most amazing YouTube videos that I have ever watched is "How the Universe Is Way Bigger Than You Think." Last time I checked, it had more than 23 million views. In my opinion, it should be required viewing for any leader who has an inflated ego. The video shows, with great mathematical accuracy, how small we are as individual human beings in relation to our earth, universe, and the greater cosmos.

As a humble leader, you aren't just aware that you need others' help and ideas; you are also aware of your insignificance in the universe. You may have worked incessantly with your team to develop a new product line that will significantly increase revenue for your organization for years to come, but in the grand scheme of things, your impact is insignificant, and you need to be aware of that.

This dimension of leadership is often referred to as "metaphysical humility," an attitude that enables you to acknowledge your nothingness in the world. This nothingness can be appreciated in terms of how powerful God is or how large the universe is, but it can also be realized by simply observing nature or contemplating history. Arrogance can sometimes make you feel like you are the center of the universe, but when you realize how connected everything is and how small and insignificant you are, you can truly develop your humility—and, in so doing, perhaps paradoxically, you become a fuller person: "When we lack connection to anything larger or bigger than us, it is like a piece of our soul is gone," as the young philosopher Ryan Holiday wrote in his remarkable book *Ego Is the Enemy*.

Please note, though, that transcendence is not a call for surrender, laziness, or relinquishing action. It is about understanding your small role but still doing it to the best of your abilities in a humble and ambitious way. You may not matter much in the grand scheme of things, but you have an important role to play in your small corner of the universe.

Humility and...

The title of the book you have in your hands is *Humbitious*, not *Humble*. The reason I chose this title, other than its catchiness and the hope that it will help with sales, is that I believe leaders can't just be humble and still hope to achieve high performance. They need to complement humility with ambition and several other important traits—as we will soon reveal.

"Humbitious" is not a term that I made up (although I really wish I had). It was coined by Jane Harper, director of internet technology and operations at IBM. Harper is credited for many achievements at IBM, and one of them is a summer internship called Extreme Blue. While the program was highly competitive and attracted smart and ambitious computer programmers and MBA students, it emphasized humility and collaboration above all. A manual offered a warning to young interns who were finishing the program: "When you leave Extreme Blue and join another group at IBM (or any other company for that matter), we will be watching. And if we find out that you are making the program look like we are producing a bunch of arrogant wanna-bes, we will forget we ever knew you. Be ambitious. Be a leader. But do not belittle others in your pursuit of your ambitions." Throughout her career, Harper strived to make sure that any leader associated with IBM displayed humbitious behaviors.

The idea that humility needs to be coupled with other positive traits in order to lead to high performance is well supported by evidence. In the classic management book *Good to Great*, Jim Collins and his research team set out to study thousands of companies in an effort to understand what sets great companies apart from merely good ones. They identified eleven "great" companies that were able to sustain superior financial performance over a long period of time. While the researchers were mainly looking for organizational—not individual—factors, one common aspect between these organizations was that they were led by a specific type of CEO that the researchers called a "Level 5 leader." This leadership style was based on humility combined with fierce determination.

Collins observed, "We were surprised, really shocked, to discover the type of leadership required for turning a good company into a great one... Compared to high-profile leaders with big personalities, who make headlines and become celebrities, the good-to-great leaders seem to have come from Mars." This paradox, Collins argues, is the "yin and yang" of leadership: Level 5 leaders are humble and ambitious, but their ambition is for the organization, not for themselves. They have no appetite for seeking attention, but they have an unwavering resolve to produce long-term performance for the collective. They demonstrate professional will through taking ownership of poor results, giving credit to others for good results, and setting the standards for building great organizations.

While Collins's research is almost two decades old, and some of the "great" organizations in the study, such as Circuit

City and Wells Fargo, haven't been so great recently, it remains the most influential research-based work on humility in leadership. It is one of the reasons why I became interested in the topic years ago and why I have dedicated the last eight years of my career to better understanding humility. Academics and researchers like me have spent a lot of time investigating which traits, other than professional will and fierce determination, are needed to complement humility in leadership.

First and foremost, it is critical to understand that competence is a must. While we saw earlier that humble leaders need to understand their weaknesses and admit their limitations, they also need to strive to achieve a high level of technical competence. This is a non-negotiable. You will lose all credibility if you show serious flaws in necessary job-related skills: a nurse manager cannot show humility to their team unless they display a deep proficiency in understanding the protocols of patient care, for example. In short, they need to "know their stuff." In one of his studies, Brad Owens looked at employees working in teams to understand the "synergistic interaction" between humility and competence. The results showed that teams experimented freely with new ideas and performed highly on important tasks only when their leaders were humble and competent.

Moreover, as we saw with Jacinda Ardern's example, taking swift action to deal with impending challenges is another necessary supplement to humility. A study of Portuguese managers and employees concluded that leaders who demonstrated humility but retreated into the background were not able to effectively engage employees in their work. However, when leaders combined humility with action—such as sharing information, coaching and mentoring others, providing direction and accountability, and establishing frameworks to ensure consistent behaviors—they were able to improve the vigor, absorption, and dedication felt by their employees.

This is not a novel idea. Robert Greenleaf, the AT&T executive credited with introducing the notion of "servant leadership," noted long ago that this approach can have an impact only if it balances a moral concern for serving people (humility) with the ability to mobilize them for performance (action). Ardern showed great empathy for the community in the aftermath of Christchurch, but she demonstrated action by working with local communities, holding social media sites accountable, and mobilizing parliament members to enact meaningful changes in gun laws.

Magnanimity

One important idea that surfaces repeatedly in the study of humble leadership is that humility and greatness create a powerful combination for leaders striving to make a lasting impact. In this context, greatness is referred to as "magnanimity." These days, magnanimity is usually used as synonymous with generosity, but the classic definition is a bit broader. According to Aristotle, magnanimity is the virtue of action. It is not just about aspiring to greatness, but also about attaining it. The great Greek philosopher reasoned that the magnanimous person practices virtue and, therefore, considers themself worthy of great things and honor.

Ancient theologians did not see any contradiction between these ambitious aspirations and humility. Thomas Aquinas argued that "a twofold virtue is necessary with regard to the difficult good: one, to temper and restrain the mind, lest it tend to high things immoderately; and this belongs to the virtue of humility; and another to strengthen the mind against despair, and urge it on to the pursuit of great things according to right reason; and this is magnanimity." With humility, you can have a clear understanding of yourself and your abilities. With that, you are able to perfect these abilities so you can achieve virtue and honor. In this sense, magnanimity and humility are two sides of the same coin: you need to trust in your own greatness (magnanimity) without losing sight of the fact that you owe that greatness to supportive people, positive forces, and favorable events (humility). You cannot become great if you are not prepared to serve others. And it is precisely in serving others that you become magnanimous.

Confidence is another key trait that pulls your followers towards you. Employees want to follow confident leaders who are decisive and have a strong sense of direction and vision. However, as leadership expert Karin Hurt notes, "confidence, without humility, can be dangerous" because it can significantly limit the effectiveness of a leader. Confident leaders who lack humility may stay the course, but they don't seek crucial input from others. They may get others to follow them, but they don't get their full support. In a recent exchange, Hurt, the founder of Let's Grow Leaders and a former Verizon Wireless executive, explained to me that while sometimes people think of confidence as the opposite of humility, we need to understand that it is an "*and* proposition." When you have the confidence to set an audacious vision coupled with the humility to know your vulnerabilities and surround yourself with people who will challenge you, then you have a powerful combination.

When you combine high confidence and high humility, you become an "enabler leader." You are not worried about being taken advantage of, because you have the confidence to speak up for yourself. You are secure enough in your own abilities that your focus is not directed towards receiving praise for yourself. Instead, you focus on the wellbeing of others, and you give credit to them for achievements. You lead for the long run and to contribute to the greater good. True confidence means that you become strong in your humility.

Don't Be a Pawn

One of the cool things I get to do as part of my job as a university professor is take time off from my classes and periodically embed myself in organizations in order to observe leadership behaviors and inform my teaching and research. We call these opportunities "faculty fellowships," and we greatly enjoy them. During my faculty fellowship in the summer of 2019, I spent two weeks at Medical City Healthcare, a division of Hospital Corporation of America (HCA). With 211 hospitals, HCA is the largest health system in the world. And Medical City Healthcare is HCA's highest performing division.

For the period of the fellowship, I interviewed leaders at all levels, visited hospitals and corporate offices, and attended numerous top strategic meetings as a fly on the wall. When I met with Erol Akdamar, the energetic division president, I asked him what traits he looks for when selecting CEOs for the fourteen hospitals that he operates. Without hesitation, he said, "Humble, hungry, and smart." He explained that he needs his top leaders to think of themselves less and to think of others more, to be focused on "hyper growth" and excellence, and to be not just book-smart, but also relationship-smart. Every other leader whom I interviewed at the various hospitals at Medical City described their vision of a high-performing leader with those exact same three terms.

Humble, hungry, and smart are the three traits of leaders that were popularized by best-selling author and management expert Patrick Lencioni in his insightful book *The Ideal Team Player*. You won't be surprised to learn that the book is required reading at Medical City Healthcare and at several other HCA divisions. In it, Lencioni argues that, when selecting team players and leaders in organizations, humility is the most important quality to look for. He views humility as the ability to accurately self-assess, to give credit to others, and to build trust. However, humble people who are only humble without working hard or building relationships with others are not effective; Lencioni calls this type of employee a "pawn." While admired for their personal qualities, pawns do not get the job done.

That's why humility needs to be complemented with a strong work ethic (hunger) and emotional intelligence (smarts). Lencioni uses clever labels to describe the other types of people who possess one or two, but not all, of these three qualities. A hungry-only type of person is a "bulldozer," while a smart-only one is a "charmer." A team member who combines humility and hunger but not smarts is an "accidental mess-maker": Lencioni explains that this person means well and works hard, but is not able to get others to work with them, thereby creating extra work for everyone due to the "political messes" they create. A "lovable slacker" is humble and smart, but not hungry; they know themselves well and collaborate with others, but they do only the minimum and never put in the extra effort needed to complete projects on time. "Lovable slackers" tend to be great interviewees but lousy employees.

However, the most dangerous type of combination that Lencioni warns every manager about is the "skillful politician."

This type of individual knows how to get others to do what they want and will put forth every effort required to succeed. But the hunger and smarts are not tempered by humility, and so this individual will stop at nothing to execute their agenda. In the words of Frank Underwood in *House of Cards*: "For those of us climbing to the top of the food chain, there can be no mercy. There is but one rule: hunt or be hunted." Lencioni's advice, which is followed closely by the leaders at Medical City Healthcare, is not to settle for one or two qualities. If you want to be highly effective, you need to develop your humility, work ethic, and emotional intelligence.

Steve 2.0

I hope that, by now, humility and ambition are looking more and more like naturally complementary traits. Humility can actually be used in the service of ambition, as long as the ambition is not just for the self, but also for the team and the organization. Surprisingly, recent research has shown that leaders can also benefit from combining humility not just with ambition, but also with narcissism. But before we examine that evidence, let's go back to the late 1970s and turn our attention to an emerging computer company.

Imagine working with someone who is preoccupied with his own brilliance. He tears your ideas down in front of others and takes credit for them if they turn out well. He lacks self-awareness, he is un-empathetic, and he controls and manipulates. That's what working for Steve Jobs felt like when Apple was first formed in 1976. He threw frequent tantrums and didn't hesitate to yell at his employees. It is well established that Jobs displayed strong signs of narcissism, with some psychologists even suggesting that he suffered from narcissistic personality disorder.

After a power struggle with then-Apple president and CEO John Sculley, Jobs left the company in 1985 and went on to found computer company NeXT, Inc. and Pixar. When Apple bought NeXT about ten years later, Jobs came back to the company that he co-founded and became its CEO once again. During this second stint, though, Jobs revealed a different leadership style. He was more introspective about his limitations, more open-minded to others' suggestions, and more appreciative of the talented people with whom he worked. In a speech that he gave at Stanford University in 2005, he reflected, "I didn't see it then, but it turned out that getting fired from Apple was the best thing that could have ever happened to me. The heaviness of being successful was replaced by the lightness of being a beginner again, less sure about everything. It freed me to enter one of the most creative periods of my life ... I'm pretty sure none of this would have happened if I hadn't been fired from Apple. It was awful tasting medicine, but I guess the patient needed it."

What is interesting about Jobs's leadership style in this second stint at Apple—let's call it Steve 2.0—is that it appears to be more humble. Certainly, he was still a narcissist, but the narcissism was tempered by humility. If you're finding this hard to believe, you're not alone. Narcissism, with its excessive self-love and self-centeredness, appears to be totally incompatible with the traits of humility that we have talked about. Humble narcissism looks to be an impossible combination—but let me explain how it is possible. Many observers believe that it was exactly this unusual combination that allowed Jobs to lead Apple to becoming the most successful company in the world. His narcissism drove him to be confident in his abilities, willing to take bold risks, and persistent in the pursuit of the goals that he set for himself and for the company. But his newly acquired humility allowed him to be more self-aware, a better collaborator, and a more effective leader overall.

Now let's examine the research that supports this argument. In a recent study, Brad Owens and his colleagues tested the hypothesis that humility could counterbalance the effects of narcissism in leaders. They asked employees working in a large health insurance company in the United States to assess the humility of the leaders for whom they worked. They also asked them whether they perceived those leaders as effective in doing their jobs and whether they felt engaged in their own work. The authors discovered that self-described narcissistic leaders were perceived as more effective, created higher engagement among their followers, and drove them to higher performance *only* when they displayed high humility. In other words, when leader humility was high, leader narcissism led to positive outcomes; but, when humility was low, leader narcissism was not conducive to good employee performance. More recently, a study conducted among employees and business-school graduates in China reached a similar conclusion: leader narcissism and humility can coexist harmoniously and enable leaders to create innovative cultures in their firms.

So how do humility and narcissism, two traits that are on the opposite ends of the same spectrum, coexist in a leader and work together to nurture high performance? Since humble leaders recognize their own flaws and imperfections, and since narcissists believe they are unique and better than everyone else, it seems like humble narcissists can enjoy the best of both worlds. When you balance narcissism with humility, you tend to set audacious goals for your organization and believe that you can achieve them, but you also know your own limitations and are willing to learn from previous mistakes. Wharton professor and organizational psychologist Adam Grant recently discussed how this powerful and unlikely combination can work: "Narcissism gives you the confidence to believe you can achieve great things... But alone, narcissism is dangerous. Narcissists tend to be overconfident. They're prone to dismissing criticism and falling victim to flattery. They surround themselves with yes-men and take unnecessary risks. Adding humility prevents capriciousness and complacency. It helps you remember that you're human. Humble narcissists have grand ambitions, but they don't feel entitled to them. They don't deny their weaknesses; they work to overcome them."

This suggests that if you are a narcissist and can find a way to inject some humility into your leadership style, you can avoid the derailments typically associated with narcissism and become a more effective leader. With humility and narcissism, you can tell yourself, "I can achieve so much in my role and in my career, but I can always learn and improve." From now on, every time you grab your iPhone, you ought to be thankful that Steve Jobs stumbled across humble narcissism.

What Next?

Humility in leadership means understanding yourself, your relationship with others, and your place in the universe. As a leader, there are a few behaviors you can start practicing to display more humbitiousness:

- Trust in your own greatness (magnanimity) without losing sight that you owe that greatness to supportive people, positive forces, and favorable events (humility).

- Have the confidence to set an audacious vision coupled with the humility to know your vulnerabilities and surround yourself with people who will challenge you.

- Work on being humble, hungry, and smart at the same time.

- If you have narcissistic tendencies, develop ways to inject some humility into your leadership style. If you are too humble, find ways to develop some healthy self-confidence and strong ambition.

In the next chapter, we will look at recent studies linking humility with outcomes in individuals, teams, and organizations.

— 2 —

The Benefits of
Humble Leadership

Pride hurts, humility benefits;
this is the rule of nature.
SHUJING, CHAPTER 3, VERSE 20

Sipping the Teacup

The game clock showed thirty minutes and thirty-nine seconds. The score was tied at 1-1. A long diagonal pass came from the back; a midfielder controlled it and floated it into a perfectly weighted cross inside the penalty box. Alex Morgan, celebrating her thirtieth birthday, leaped over her marker and placed a strong header past the goalkeeper. USA: 2, England: 1.

"Happy birthday, Alex Morgan!" screamed the TV commentator as Morgan ran in celebration. Then, in a moment that seemed to stand still, Morgan stopped, raised her right hand, and sipped tea from an imaginary cup. Then her teammates jumped over to congratulate her, and the moment was over.

That image of Alex Morgan with her extended pinky celebrating the winning goal in the semifinal game for the

U.S. women's national soccer team became one of the most iconic and controversial images of the 2019 World Cup. It also revealed a lot about how the world thinks about humility, confidence, and arrogance.

The English were outraged. How dare the Americans mock them? A former English player said to journalists that evening, "We love our tea in England ... so I think it's a little bit distasteful." The English media reacted as if Morgan had killed the queen.

What made the Morgan celebration one of the most talked-about incidents at the World Cup was that it fed the narrative that English and other European journalists had begun weaving from the beginning of the tournament. Many of the U.S. players were superstars, and some had millions of Instagram followers. All of that stardom must have gone to their heads and made them intolerably arrogant, the journalists claimed. The English newspapers, public, and even players and coaches waged a daily propaganda war against the Americans, calling them smug and entitled. What exactly happened over the span of three weeks for a group of hard-working and skilled soccer players to be labeled as the most arrogant team in history?

The United States had started the tournament a couple of weeks earlier by beating a weak Thailand side by a record score of 13-0, and by allegedly "over-celebrating" the goals. A few days later, after they changed the lineup and still beat Chile 3-0, thus securing qualification to the second round, one of the American players told journalists, "We have the best team in the world, and the second-best team in the world." The story about "those arrogant Americans" started to grow legs and circulate all around press offices and social media platforms in England and across the world.

Let's stop to separate fact from fiction. When the U.S. players ran up the score against Thailand and joyfully high-fived and hugged each other in celebration, they weren't being arrogant. In fact, they were being respectful of the Thai team by treating the game as the serious World Cup challenge that it was, playing hard from the first to the last minute. Had they eased off, showing off their skills or passing the ball around, then that would likely have been considered more disrespectful to their opponents. It would also have been foolish—goal difference is an important tiebreaker at the World Cup. And when the American player stated that the United States has at least two excellent players in every position, she wasn't being arrogant; she was stating how confident she was in her and her teammates' abilities. There is a difference between confidence and arrogance.

In fact, the U.S. team's style of play throughout the tournament, and especially in the knockout-stage wins against Spain, France, and England, was the furthest thing from arrogance. If the U.S. team had been arrogant, they would not have taken their opponents as seriously and would have assumed that they could win just by showing up. The evidence shows that they did the opposite: the way they played looked more like "aggressive humility." They took the lead early in most games and then defended with great resolve for long periods of time before securing the win; they meticulously prepared and changed their approach depending on the opponent they faced; they knew their own strengths and weaknesses and used them to win in every game. Alex Morgan and her teammates were able to celebrate over and over again that summer because they had self-awareness, grit, and humility in viewing themselves and their opponents accurately. That is pure humbition.

Before the England game, the soft-spoken American coach explained in simple words the difference between perceptions about her team and the reality: "It's important that our team has confidence. I don't think in any way this is an arrogant team. I think this team knows they have to earn everything, that we've got tough opponents ... and we have to earn every right to advance in this tournament." Other players echoed those same sentiments: "We have the utmost respect for England and every team that we faced and every team that we will face forever and ever. That's just part of the DNA of this squad." It is impossible to be arrogant when you respect your opponents and work hard to beat them.

The U.S. women's national team went on to beat the Netherlands in the final game and win back-to-back World Cup trophies. This historical achievement demonstrated that teams that approach their challenges with humility can set themselves up for success, regardless of what their critics say. (And it must also be noted that gender clearly played a role in the criticism levied against the American team. There is ample evidence that women deal with similar double standards all the time—but that's another book that has already been written. Please refer to the excellent book *Why Do So Many Incompetent Men Become Leaders?* by Tomas Chamorro-Premuzic.) So in this chapter, we're going to look at how humility is connected to positive performance outcomes, for individuals, teams, and organizations.

"I Believe I Am Very Humble"

In order to study humility, we need first to measure it. This can be difficult. Earlier research studying humility asked people to rate themselves on how humble they were; you may not be surprised to learn that the truly humble tended to rate themselves low on humility, while the arrogant were inclined to overestimate how humble they were. As is often said, the truly humble never know that they are humble. So before we inspect the various studies linking humility to performance, we need to discuss how humility is measured.

Since, as researchers have noted, humility may be "simply unamenable to self-report methods," different ways have been devised to accurately measure it. The most popular tool for measuring humility in leadership is the one developed by Brad Owens and his colleagues—I referred to it in Chapter 1. Based on their definition of humility as consisting of a willingness to see the self accurately, an appreciation of others' strengths and contributions without feeling threatened, teachability and openness to learning and feedback, and low self-focus, they developed a tool to measure *expressed humility*. Expressed humility occurs in interpersonal interactions and is observable by other people, which makes it easy to measure using others' ratings. Followers and team members are asked to evaluate their leader on nine items:

1   This person actively seeks feedback, even if it is critical.

2   This person admits it when they don't know how to do something.

3   This person acknowledges when others have more knowledge and skills than him- or herself.

4   This person takes notice of others' strengths.

5   This person often compliments others on their strengths.

6   This person shows appreciation for the unique contributions of others.

7   This person is willing to learn from others.

8   This person is open to the ideas of others.

9   This person is open to the advice of others.

This simple nine-question tool is the most widely used instrument for assessing humble leadership in research conducted across the world.

Acing the Final Exam

Suppose you are a student enrolled in a tough upper-level course. You are struggling to keep up with the professor and to understand the complex concepts being covered. You take the midterm exam and get a "C." You would do anything to improve your score on the final exam. What one trait, more than anything else, can predict whether you will be able to overcome this challenge and turn things around?

This is one of the questions that Owens and his team asked themselves when they designed their research. They invited 144 students enrolled in a management course at the University of Washington to be part of an experiment in which they were asked to work in teams on a final report and presentation and to take various psychological assessments, for example, a self-efficacy assessment and a conscientiousness assessment. Halfway through the course, the students rated each other on humility using Owens's previously described tool. Everyone enrolled in the course took a general mental ability test as well.

The results showed that, more than self-efficacy, conscientiousness, or mental ability, it was humility that best predicted each student's performance in the course. In other words, students who were rated higher on humility by their team members did better in the course than students who were rated lower, and humility was more strongly associated with getting a good grade than all the other factors measured in the study. The reason behind this remarkable finding is that humble students are able to accurately self-assess, which means that they are more realistic about how much time and effort is required to fulfill performance expectations, and consequently are less likely to miss deadlines and sacrifice the quality of their work. Moreover, humble students appreciate the strengths of others and are more likely to notice high performers on their teams and in the class and attempt to model their behaviors.

Owens and his colleagues also noticed that humility was not only a strong predictor of overall performance, but also the main factor affecting improvement of test scores between the midterm and final exam. Since humble students were open to feedback, they were more likely to learn from their mistakes and take remedial action after an initial low performance, which enabled them to achieve higher performance later.

Even more interestingly, humility significantly compensated for low mental ability among some of the students. In other words, students with lower mental abilities and higher humility performed equivalently to those with higher general mental ability and lower humility. To better understand this finding, let's say we have two students in a class, Alexandra and Donald. Alexandra scored lower on the mental ability test but was rated higher on humility by her teammates than Donald. Let's assume that Donald earned an 85/100 on the midterm, while Alexandra received only a 79/100. By understanding her own abilities, listening to her professor's suggestions, and asking others for help, Alexandra displayed a humility that allowed her to outperform Donald and earn 87/100 on the final exam. This clearly suggests that people can benefit from finding ways to develop more humility in order to improve their overall performance.

Not only is humility beneficial for student performance, it also contributes positively to how students feel about themselves. Baylor University professor Wade Rowatt and his team studied a group of 135 undergraduate students and asked them to take assessments related to humility and several measures of personality self-concept. They also asked an acquaintance of each student to rate the student's humility. They found that humble students were more satisfied with their own life, had higher self-esteem, and were generally more grateful and agreeable than non-humble students. Moreover, students displaying humility were less likely to be neurotic and pessimistic, show signs of depression, or report poor health. Similarly, a study conducted at the University of Gdańsk in Poland found strong connections between different aspects of humility and subjective wellbeing, life aspirations, and happiness among adults. In particular, individuals who acknowledged their own limitations and accepted reality as it was were more likely to have meaningful relationships and to demonstrate personal growth and good health, while those who used their failures to improve themselves had better overall health.

The Water Carriers

Carla Overbeck. Carles Puyol. Tim Duncan.

If you're an avid sports fan, then the images these names bring to your mind are of celebrations and trophies—lots of trophies. Carla Overbeck captained the U.S. women's soccer team between 1996 and 1999 ("The '99ers") and won the World Cup and Olympic gold medal with a record of 84 wins, 6 ties, and only 6 losses. Carles Puyol was the captain of the best Barcelona soccer team in history. Between 2008 and 2013, he and his teammates collected fifteen major trophies, including four Spanish LaLiga titles and two European Champions League titles (arguably the highest honor in club soccer in the world). Tim Duncan led the San Antonio Spurs (my hometown team) over two decades, during which the team won five NBA rings, reached the playoffs nineteen straight times, and posted a record 71 percent winning rate.

The common thread among these amazing captains, other than the successes they had in their fields, is that they were all humble and fiercely ambitious leaders. Sportswriter and leadership columnist Sam Walker refers to this type of captain as the "water carrier." In his hugely entertaining and methodologically thorough book *The Captain Class*, Walker set out to identify the best teams in the history of all competitions (think *Good to Great* applied to sports). According to Walker's strict criteria and detailed calculations, only seventeen teams were dominant enough over a long period of time while playing against the world's top competition to qualify to be in this top tier: the top 0.1 percent in terms of winning and achievement among thousands of excellent teams. The '99ers, Barcelona, and the Spurs were three of those elite teams. Other notable names on the list included the New York Yankees of 1949-1953, the Boston Celtics of 1956-1969, and the New England Patriots of 2001-2018. The aforementioned U.S. women's soccer team will be a strong contender to squeeze into this group in the near future.

The main finding from Walker's examination is that the most crucial ingredient in a team that achieves and sustains historic greatness is not the amount of resources available to it, the experience of its coach, or the loyalty of its fans. It is the character of its captain. All seventeen top-tier teams had a humble and ambitious captain whose presence coincided with the long winning streak and whose absence or retirement corresponded with the team becoming average once again. The majority of sports fans believe that an elite team should have a superstar player (such as a Michael Jordan, Alex Morgan, or Cristiano Ronaldo) in order to dominate its opponents. And while having the best player of their generation can certainly increase the chances of winning big trophies, Walker's research shows that, for a team to become elite over a sustainable period of time, the most important factor is not a GOAT (Greatest Of All Time) type of player, but a captain who leads from the shadows.

Walker refers to these captains as "water carriers" because, except for Duncan and a few others, they were not especially gifted players. Rather, they were average players who carried the water, so to speak, to their more technically skilled teammates and helped them shine and win. Carla Overbeck, for example, scored only seven goals in her entire soccer career. As soon as she got the ball, her first instinct was to pass it to a teammate who was more skilled and had a better chance of scoring and helping the team. While most of the captains were ordinary players in terms of their skill levels, they had a fanatical commitment to winning that was not matched by any other player on the team.

It is interesting to note that the captains of these elite teams displayed very similar characteristics to the Level 5 leaders described in *Good to Great*. They combined selflessness with determination. They lowered themselves in relation to their teammates in order to earn the moral authority to drive them forward in tough moments. They led by serving others. Tim Duncan, for example, always put himself in the service of the team, sacrificing his individual numbers in order to set up plays that allowed the team to perform better. In 2013, he agreed to cut his pay by half in order to allow the Spurs to have enough financial flexibility under the NBA's salary cap to attract other players who could benefit the team. In the age of self-centered superstars, Duncan exhibited an extreme humility that was unmatched.

Humble Hannah

Humble leaders are important not only for sport teams, but also for organizational teams. To better understand the research evidence related to humility in teams, let's meet Hannah (a fictional character based on a real executive I know). Hannah is the senior vice president of strategy at a large service company. She has extensive experience in strategy, having spent the last twenty years of her career in various executive positions, planning and directing large-scale operations. She is an admired leader, but the one quality that sets her apart is her humility. In her communications with her team, she always talks about the team's achievements and uses "we" and "us." In individual and group meetings, she tends to listen more than she speaks. When she sees someone in the hallway, whether it's another executive or a housekeeper, she stops to greet them and ask about their family. She constantly praises her team members' strengths and contributions, and she is always open to new ideas and feedback. While very competent, Hannah is not hesitant to share her shortcomings with her team or to admit when she makes a mistake.

As a result of her humble leadership style, Hannah creates *collective humility* within her team. Collective humility is a group-level phenomenon characterized by team members emulating their humble leader's behavior by willingly admitting their mistakes and limitations, openly acknowledging each other's contributions and strengths, and showing receptiveness to new ideas and feedback. When Hannah behaves in a humble way, she is modeling how to grow for her team members. As they observe their leader's willingness to learn and be vulnerable, her team members start feeling that their own growth and improvement is not only legitimate, but also necessary. When she admits her mistakes and limitations, Hannah provides the opportunity for a *collective promotion focus* to emerge, which means the team becomes focused on striving to achieve its highest potential. Team members become motivated to focus on what they can collectively achieve, not on what can go wrong. As Hannah acknowledges her team members' strengths and contributions, she motivates them to focus on maximizing the team's performance. And as she models teachability, she gives them the ability to focus on new attainments. As a result, the team displays a *growth climate* in which it constantly strives to attain higher achievements than it has in the past.

Another great benefit of Hannah's approach is that it creates a positive psychological state within the team characterized by efficacy, optimism, hope, and resilience, commonly referred to as *psychological capital* (PsyCap for short, if you want to impress people at a party hosted by academics). Team members feel efficacious in that they have the confidence to put in the necessary effort to deal with challenging tasks. They become optimistic and believe that they can make positive contributions towards goals and plans. Their hope drives them to persevere towards goals and, when necessary, to redirect their paths in order to succeed. Moreover, they become more resilient and can bounce back from setbacks and adversity. Building on this, the team is better equipped to align specific member skills to precise team tasks and to give each member the chance to do the things that they feel they can do best (*team task allocation effectiveness*). Not surprisingly, Hannah's team constantly exceeds expectations and provides great value to the organization.

What I just shared is based on thorough research that was conducted in the last few years among hundreds of teams in organizations in China, Portugal, Singapore, and the United States. The following figure provides a schematic representation of how humble leadership can drive a team's culture and performance.

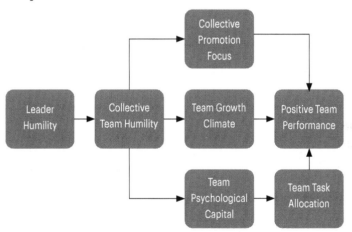

Kindergarteners and MBAs

The kindergarteners couldn't contain their excitement. As soon as they were given the signal, they started playing with the spaghetti sticks and marshmallows. On the other side of the room, recently graduated MBAs were nervously sizing each other up. Groups of CEOs and lawyers also looked hesitant and tense. They were all part of the "Marshmallow Challenge," an experiment used to test rapid prototyping that was designed by author and Autodesk Fellow Tom Wujec. Each group (the kindergartners, the MBAs, the CEOs, and the lawyers) were given twenty sticks of spaghetti, a yard of string, strips of Scotch tape, and a marshmallow. They were allocated eighteen minutes and asked to build the highest possible structure with the marshmallow on top.

The kindergartners built the highest structure, at twenty-eight inches. The CEOs came in next, followed by the lawyers. The worst performing team was the MBAs, with a measly ten-inch structure. Why? One explanation is that the kindergarteners, unlike the other groups, have curiosity and creativity and, most importantly, are not afraid to fail. The instant the experiment began, they started building and failing, but they couldn't have cared less about what everyone around them thought. The MBAs, on the other hand, started with trying to gauge power and establish dominance. They competed to emerge as an informal leader for the team. They nervously planned while making sure not to step on each other's toes. They didn't feel safe to experiment and mess up. Terrified to fail in front of their peers, they waited a full ten minutes before they actually started building the tower. As a result, they performed worse—far worse—than the kindergarteners.

What the kindergarteners displayed in this experiment, and what the other teams lacked to various degrees, was *psychological safety*. Since the creation of mankind, humans have belonged to groups, because belonging means protection and safety. Nowadays, when we join a new group at work, we look for cues that assure us we are safe. This way we can stop worrying about threats and start making connections with others in the group. As we make those connections, we start feeling psychologically safe. When researchers observe a safe team, what they see is that its members are willing to experiment and are not afraid to fail. Moreover, everyone talks and listens in roughly equal measure. Individuals maintain high levels of eye contact and their conversations and gestures are energetic. They communicate directly with one another, not just with the team leader, and they carry on side conversations within the team.

Amy Edmondson, a Harvard Business School professor, is credited with introducing the concept of psychological safety into the management literature. At a 2019 research conference in Boston, she quipped that while she had been conducting research on the topic for the last twenty years, it wasn't until Google discovered its importance that the concept became known in the popular literature. One of her earlier research studies was conducted with her student Ingrid Nembhard in neonatal intensive care units. They discovered that leaders who invited and appreciated others' contributions and included them in important discussions and decisions—which, as we have discussed before, are humbitious behaviors—were more likely to create a psychologically safe environment in their units. This, in turn, resulted in a greater involvement of unit employees in quality-improvement efforts, an important measure of performance in healthcare organizations.

Other researchers did a study where participants would receive small payments for doing human intelligence tasks such as validating data and participating in surveys. They found that leader humility affected psychological safety and engagement in two main ways. First, humble leaders emphasized to their team members that making mistakes is normal and necessary for development. This helped legitimize their followers' development. Second, humble leaders stressed that feeling unsure about certain tasks and situations is normal. This validated uncertainty, and employees felt more comfortable voicing their doubts. They sensed that they could be themselves without fear of negative ramifications, and they could fully engage in their work.

As we saw when looking at Humble Hannah, humble leaders significantly improve their teams' performance by creating positive conditions. One of the underlying aspects of these conditions is that team members feel comfortable voicing their opinions, experimenting, and failing. In this environment, team members believe that their ideas are welcomed and built upon, and don't fear ridicule or punishment if their opinions are different. These conditions unleash *knowledge sharing* within the team: team members share know-how from work experiences with each other and exchange success and failure stories.

Moving from Disgruntled to Gruntled

"The best bosses are humble bosses," read the headline of a 2018 article in *The Wall Street Journal*. The article proposed that, "after decades of screening potential leaders for charm and charisma, some employers are realizing they've been missing one of the most important traits of all: humility." Surprisingly, hyper-competitive Wall Street companies were starting to appreciate the importance of humility. Studies examining humble leadership in academic journals started to appear around 2005, and they have exponentially increased in the last few years. Brad Owens of BYU believes there are several factors behind this interest in studying humility. "My guess is that this interest is driven in part by perceived need in society," he told me. "In our hyper-connected world, stories of arrogant, overconfident, entitled, narcissistic leaders seem to be widely publicized ... The increase over the last five years is also likely due to having measures and a more solid theoretical foundation for leader humility."

Leader humility has an important effect on employee engagement—a key predictor of organizational performance. It is well documented that a large proportion of employees do not feel highly engaged: they are psychologically unattached to their work, they contribute the minimum required, and they will not hesitate to leave for even a slightly better offer. While leaders claim that they are highly inspiring, the majority of employees proclaim that their leaders and organizations do not engage them at all.

In a very interesting take on employee engagement, Dan Cable, professor of organizational behavior at London Business School, argues that there is a biological explanation for why employees feel disengaged at work. Drawing on extensive neuroscientific research, he demonstrates that, as human beings, we have *seeking systems*—deeply ingrained parts of our brains that crave learning and exploration. When organizations and leaders suppress these seeking systems through autocratic leadership, steep hierarchies, and rigid rules, we lose our zest for work and become disengaged. Cable believes that leader humility, among other factors, can play a major role in improving employee engagement. He argues that the key performance indicators and reward/penalty systems that are prevalent in most organizations cause only small changes in behaviors and do not motivate employees in the long run.

What really stimulates people is learning new things and experimenting with new ways. That is why you need to model these behaviors in order to move the needle on employee engagement.

Cable relates the story of a Chinese bank that was historically dominated by traditional management systems and top-down leadership. Under this old-fashioned management approach, one banker commented, "if I admit lack of knowledge, then I am punished so I can't learn. I am rewarded for confidently faking that I know best when I don't." One morning, a humble corporate executive decided to try something different. He showed up early at a local branch and surprised the employees by serving them breakfast. He then held small huddles to ask for their input on how to improve the performance of the branch. While the employees were hesitant at first, they quickly warmed up to the executive and his humble approach. They saw it as an invitation to share their creative thoughts and learn together. The executive enabled them to move towards their full potential by growing and trying new ideas. As a leader, rather than just talking about the importance of learning and experimenting, you need to show your employees how to develop by acknowledging mistakes and limitations and being open to listening, observing, and learning by doing. This style of leadership can trigger your employees' seeking systems.

Leader humility, by enabling engagement, can be an essential tool in competing for talent. Employees bring more of themselves to work when their leaders activate their seeking systems by placing a priority on providing tangible and emotional support as they explore new ways to improve themselves and their teams. When you listen and give your employees the chance to explore their environments and discover new things, even disgruntled employees can reactivate their seeking systems. This results not only in better products and services, but also in more enthusiasm and zest. People stop dreading their jobs and come alive at work. In the words of fictional Dunder Mifflin regional manager Michael Scott, employees will no longer be disgruntled; instead, they will become "gruntled."

Cable's arguments about the connection between humility and engagement have been supported by several studies in the last few years. Through fifty-five interviews with high-level executives, mid-level managers, and front-line supervisors, Brad Owens and David Hekman clarified the path by which humble leadership affects employee engagement. Humble leaders, as mentioned before, are transparent about their personal limitations and their willingness to learn from others, and are confident in presenting themselves as "works in progress." As a result, their followers feel validated in their own development efforts, since the message from the leader appears to be: "It's okay to be a work in progress here." Their engagement and motivation to do the work are unleashed, and their followers' motivations shift from just trying to meet external performance standards (such as getting a pay raise, a promotion, or praise from the boss) to more intrinsic motivations to learn, master tasks, and fulfill their potential. Humble leaders unlock and amplify those deeper yearnings, enabling their followers to go above the bare minimum when performing their tasks. One employee in the study noted, "I actually enjoy working late and going above and beyond the call of duty when [my humble leader] genuinely asks for help about something or admits they are confused about an issue."

Even when you model a small display of growth, such as asking for advice, you can motivate employees to double their efforts, while a tough display of non-humble behaviors, such as yelling at an employee, can strongly demotivate them. This was captured by another employee in the study, who observed, "When my leader shows humility and is open to what others have to say, it creates an environment of energy. I come to the meetings prepared. Rather than stepping in the room and saying, 'Okay, he's going to set the agenda and we are going to sit here and listen for an hour,' it's more interactive, we feel like we have more impact."

These interview findings are supported by large quantitative studies. Leadership experts Jack Zenger and Joe Folkman conducted 360-degree feedback assessments for 69,000 leaders at hundreds of firms all over the world. The leaders in the study rated themselves while also being evaluated by their superiors, colleagues, and subordinates (a total of 750,000 respondents) on their leadership effectiveness. Leaders who rated themselves lower than how they were rated by others (a clear sign of humility, as we showed earlier) had employee engagement scores that were more than twenty points higher than leaders who rated themselves higher than how they were rated by others. While this shows that leaders are not always good at rating themselves, it also indicates that underrating yourself is generally better than overrating yourself.

In a recent exchange, Joe Folkman provided some additional insights. He explained to me that "a humble leader always assumes the intentions of their performance is never as good as what people actually experience. They also consider, 'What could I have done to do a better job?'" Because of this developmental mindset, employees' growth is encouraged and engagement is improved. Similarly, Amy Ou, from the Hong Kong Polytechnic University, and her colleagues established, in their study of Chinese private companies, that middle managers led by humble CEOs are more engaged in their work due to the leaders' empowering style.

Humility after the Earthquake

It is no surprise that when employees are better motivated and engaged they are more likely to generate new ideas and invent solutions to problems, as we saw earlier in the research on teams. But it is important to remember that engaging in those types of proactive behaviors can be psychologically risky. If the efforts are not successful, there is a real risk that the employee will be blamed for the negative outcomes. As a humbitious leader, you need to psychologically empower your employees in order to create a safe environment for proactivity and experimentation.

In her master's thesis at the University of Twente in the Netherlands, Stella-Oriana Strüfing interviewed German organizational leaders to better understand the relationship between humble leadership and creativity. The participants related that, by showing their own weaknesses, mistakes, and limitations; spotlighting others' strengths; and modeling teachability, humble leaders unleashed their employees' engagement. This, in turn, allowed the employees to work independently and experience freedom in the execution of their tasks. When your employees have more space and feel less controlled, they feel less restricted by requirements, and they incorporate their own ideas and work more creatively.

Innovativeness is especially important for teams dealing with extreme environmental pressures, such as those experienced after major natural events and disasters or global pandemics. For example, in the aftermath of the large 2008 earthquake that hit China's Sichuan province, killing thousands and displacing millions, leaders and workers in local hospital teams had to come up with creative solutions to overcome blocked roads and malfunctioning communications systems in order to bring the injured to locations where they could be treated. Researchers at Xi'an Jiaotong University embedded themselves in medical taskforce teams to investigate the impact of leader behaviors under these tough conditions. They found that workers interacting with a humble leader were more likely to display *perspective taking*, which means they were able to see the perspective of their leaders and teammates in order to make a comprehensive evaluation of the situation. They tried to look at everybody's side of a disagreement before they made a decision, and attempted to imagine how other people felt before they criticized them. By considering all points of view, these workers were able to integrate novel ideas into how they solved logistical problems. They displayed more creativity and suggested more new ways to achieve goals than workers who reported to non-humble leaders.

Other studies have also documented the connection between leader humility and employee innovativeness, albeit through a different path than perspective taking. When you display humble behaviors, you can impact how your employees subconsciously evaluate themselves, objects, and events—a concept social scientists call *core self-evaluation* (CSE). If you are an open-minded and teachable leader, employees who interact with you will display "strong internal motivation, positive cognition and coping style, and good abilities, in addition to more positive emotions, attitudes and reaction behaviors," which are indicators of high CSE. When your employees have higher core self-evaluation, they are more likely to find problems, generate new ideas, seek creative support, and implement innovative plans.

Another possible mechanism through which leader humility impacts engagement and satisfaction is by giving employees permission to give constructive suggestions and challenge the status quo, which is referred to among social scientists as *voice behavior*. If you are a humble leader, your employees are more likely to trust that you will be fair and impartial, which creates an environment where they feel safe to affect operations and to invite other co-workers to solve problems. Moreover, your employees feel a personal sense of power in their own ability to influence you by getting you to listen to what they have to say. As a result, they are more likely to speak up with recommendations to fix things and to frequently make suggestions to improve work processes.

Experienced executive coach Lee Angus recently shared with me the story of a non-humble executive he worked with a while ago: "The CEO was always complaining that 'no one comes up with new ideas here!' I confronted him and told him that it was because of the culture of fear that he had created, where people believe it is dangerous to be wrong. Not surprisingly, he refused to listen." As a humbitious leader, in contrast, you are open to experimentation and to trying new things, since your ego is not wrapped up in being right. You model that attitude and behavior to your followers, who then adopt it as their own and end up benefiting the organization with their ideas and contributions.

Show Me the Money

Let's switch gears and talk about resilience, a quality that has been especially sought after by leaders since the recent Covid-19 pandemic. It is well established that resilience in individuals and organizations is a predictor of long-term performance. "More than education, more than experience, more than training, a person's level of resilience will determine who succeeds and who fails. That's true in the cancer ward, it's true in the Olympics, and it's true in the boardroom," wrote Diane Coutu in a seminal *Harvard Business Review* article. Since then, experts have been studying resilience to better understand its determinants and effects. Resilient people tend to be those who are naturally optimistic about life. They view setbacks as temporary ("it's going away quickly"), local ("it's just this one situation"), and changeable ("I can do something about it").

Is there a connection between leader humility and employee resilience? A recent study tested this interesting question. It found that employees working for humble leaders were more likely to display *work-related promotion focus*, a condition in which they took chances to maximize their goals for advancement and spent time envisioning how to fulfill their aspirations. They also had greater *perceived insider identity*, which means they felt very much a part of their organization and believed they were included in it. As a result, these employees were more likely to demonstrate resilience. Due in large part to their leader's humility, they were more likely to use change as an opportunity for growth and to continuously reevaluate their performance and improve the way they do their work.

Given the evidence that we have reviewed so far, it should come as no surprise that humble leadership results in better individual and organizational performance. When employees and managers feel energized, engaged, creative, and resilient, they are more likely to perform well on their work-related tasks. As a result, the whole organization performs better.

Let's now examine in more depth the connection between your style as a leader and the outcomes that your organization can achieve. When you display open-mindedness, teachability, and low self-focus, you empower your top management teams to be better integrated. The executives in these teams will be more inclined to collaborate with each other, share information freely, make joint decisions, and agree on shared visions for the organization. This enables the organization to become more fluid in dealing with changes and to display a strategic orientation characterized by a double focus on exploration (thinking outside the box) and exploitation (improving efficiency and reliability). How does that influence the financial outcomes of the organization?

In one study conducted in the computer hardware and software industries, organizations driven by humble CEOs leading well-integrated, top management teams with strong strategic orientations had better financial performance than similar organizations led by non-humble CEOs. Specifically, humble leadership was associated with a significantly higher return on assets over a twelve-month period, which suggests that this style of leadership is not just a feel-good, mushy way of leading, but is rather a realistic approach that can improve important outcomes.

Humble leadership is clearly a humane way to lead and should be adopted by leaders because it is the right thing to do. But I am very relieved (as are the CFOs with whom I speak) that it not only makes us feel better, it also significantly contributes to the bottom line. Undoubtedly, humble leadership presents a competitive advantage, as it enables leaders, top managers, and employees to have a realistic view of themselves, their organizations, and their environments. The following figure summarizes how humility affects individual and organizational outcomes.

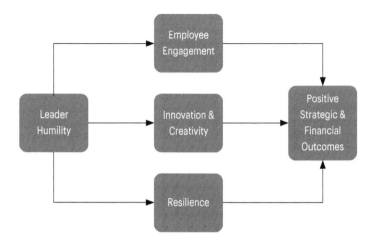

What Next?

There's no doubt that humble leadership benefits individuals, teams, and organizations; we've seen the impact of humility on how individuals and teams behave, and the organizational outcomes that result. Here are a few actions the research suggests you should take:

- Set up your team to confront challenges with humility and confidence.

- Combine selflessness with fierce determination.

- Model humility by admitting mistakes and shortcomings.

- Create psychological safety so that people don't worry about threats and feel comfortable developing deep connections with each other.

- Improve engagement by empowering employees to grow and experiment.

In the next chapter, we will look at the determinants of humility and its possible limitations.

— 3 —

Determinants and Moderators of Humble Leadership

Humility is an orientation that represents an underlying belief in one's capacity for substantial growth and self-development.

BRAD OWENS

Ditching the Big Office

Stacey Taylor was very excited: the board had chosen her as the new executive director. She had been working for a while at MET (Motivation, Education, and Training), a not-for-profit organization that provides employment training and family services to rural communities, and now she finally had the top job. It wasn't the prestige of the position that excited her, however; she just couldn't wait to start implementing new ideas to allow MET to help even more people become self-sufficient in the five states that it served.

As had been the tradition, the chair of the board offered Stacey the key to the big fancy office, where previous executive directors had sat behind the large wooden desk for the last twenty years. The office was massive: it was four times the size of any other office in the executive suite and it contained a comfortable sofa, a spacious kitchenette, and a private bathroom. MET employees jokingly compared it to the oval office. To everyone's surprise, Stacey respectfully declined the big office, and instead moved to a very nice but regular office next door. She made the decision to turn the large office into a community gathering place and conference room.

The move sent a stir throughout the organization. "The board was very concerned and shocked. They were like, 'Why are you doing this? This is the best office!' The news traveled in the organization like wildfire. The employees were also confused and skeptical," Stacey recently explained to me. She wanted to send a message to the whole organization: this is a new day. In the past, the office had been symbolic of absolute power and top-down authority. She wanted to signal that, from then on, decisions would be made based on inputs and honest dialogue. It took some time for the employees to accept Stacey's decision, but once they did, they never looked back. "Now we have different groups using the big office; it's open all the time. People use it as a space for alone time for a few minutes, as a refuge. Nothing pleases me more than when I see employees taking their lunch break there and sitting on the couch," she said. Gradually, both the board and the employees saw her decision not as a publicity stunt, but as an indicator of her humble and open leadership style.

Working with MET on their strategic plans, I have observed Stacey interact with board members with humility and respect while intentionally nudging them to make the right decisions for the organization. As a result, she has successfully led an increase of more than 40 percent in grant money received in two short years. "Humility is paramount for me. It is intentional. I choose every day to be humble in my management style. I make a conscious decision. When you have a fancy title and hundreds of employees, it is easy to put yourself on a pedestal, because you have power," she reflected to me.

I pushed her to think about what factors in her past had led her to this approach: was it her personality, upbringing, or professional experiences? "I come from a long line of tenacious, hard-working, natural born leaders," she explained. Stacey grew up outside of Thunder Bay, Ontario, a medium-sized town of a bit more than 100,000 people known for its bizarrely named "Persian donuts." Her father came to Canada from Italy at the age of nine and settled with his family in Northern Ontario. As adults, he and his sister founded a small company. Stacey's mother helped run the business; her aunts and uncles and even her grandmother worked there too. Stacey started helping out with the business when she was twelve. Her parents were raising her to be confident and resilient and to have her feet firmly planted on the ground, but also "not to take crap from anyone!" She watched all the strong women in her family work at the business and raise families effortlessly. "There was a lot of love in this multi-generational workforce. I modeled my own leadership style on this. It is communal and humble, not autocratic leadership," Stacey reflected. "There is nothing more humble than your eighty-year-old grandmother who came here with nothing and didn't speak the language working in the family business because she wanted to contribute!"

In addition to her family upbringing, Stacey believes that her experiences have also shaped her as a leader. When she worked for humble managers in the past, she thrived. However, when she worked for authoritarians who went by the principle of "because I said so," she felt stifled and couldn't be creative. "That is why I always thought that when I was the leader, I would consciously try to be humble in my leadership style. That is how I develop my people, and I help them so they can help me."

In this chapter, we will examine what factors shape leaders like Stacey to become more humble. There are some who are naturally wired by personality or predisposition to be more humble than others. That is the usual "nature" argument. But what are the "nurture" factors that may lead to a more humble leadership style, where getting results for the organization, rather than satisfying one's own ego, is the driving force?

Proving vs. Improving

Imagine this scenario for a moment: You are a young adult having a very bad day. "You go to a class that is really important to you and that you like a lot. The professor returns the midterm paper to the class. You got a C+. You're very disappointed. That evening on the way back to your home, you find that you've gotten a parking ticket. Being really frustrated, you call your best friend to share your experience but are sort of brushed off." How would you feel about that bad day, and how would you react?

When Stanford professor Carol Dweck asked people to imagine experiencing this scenario, a group of them said that they would feel like a total failure, an idiot, or a loser. Their lives would be pitiful and unfair and they would believe that all efforts are useless. They would cope with the situation by staying in bed, getting drunk, or crying. However, the other group in the study thought very differently about the same scenario. They said that while they would be upset, they would feel that they needed to study harder in class and be more careful about where to park, and they wondered if the friend was also having a bad day. They would handle the situation by looking at what questions they missed on the exam, paying or contesting the ticket, and calling the friend to discuss what is wrong.

What explains this huge discrepancy in the feelings and reactions between the two groups? Dweck attributes the difference to the mindset that people have and that shapes how they view themselves. The people in the first group who perceived the bad day as all doom and gloom have a *fixed mindset*, whereas those who were distressed by the day but still decided to directly confront the challenges, Dweck proposes, have a *growth mindset*.

These findings are not just limited to hypothetical scenarios. Based on her research findings, Dweck argues that the views we adopt can profoundly affect the way we lead our personal and professional lives. If we have a fixed mindset, we believe that our qualities are carved in stone, that we have a limited amount of intelligence, a certain personality, and a certain moral character. We are always thinking: "Will I look smart or dumb? Will I be accepted or rejected?" This creates an urgency to prove ourselves in every interaction we have with others. When we underachieve or face a bad day, we feel like utter failures and decide to stop trying. If we have a growth mindset, on the other hand, we believe that our basic qualities can be cultivated through effort. Although we understand that people may differ in their initial talents or aptitudes, we have faith that everyone can change and grow through application and experience. That doesn't mean we think everyone can become Newton or Mozart. It means we believe that a person's true potential is unknown and that much can be achieved through passion and hard work. As a result, we don't waste our time on *proving* how good we are; rather, we focus on *improving* all the time. When we face tough days or encounter difficulties, we see them as learning opportunities and jump at them head-first.

Dweck has spent the last thirty years investigating fixed and growth mindsets and their implications for parents, teachers, and leaders. Some recent research has shown the connection between the mindset a leader has and their degree of humility. For example, a study of eighty-five teams in China revealed that leaders who have growth mindsets and believe that "everyone, no matter who they are, can significantly change their basic characteristics" are more likely to be rated as humble by their followers. Leaders who have more fixed mindsets and who subscribe to the notion that "everyone is a certain kind of a person and that there is not much they can do about it" are perceived as less humble.

To better interpret these findings, let's go back to what humility is all about. One of the most important aspects of humility that we described in earlier chapters consists of being self-aware, understanding your own deficiencies, and admitting your mistakes to others. When you have a growth mindset and believe that your abilities and personality are malleable, you view your mistakes as meaningful steps for ongoing development rather than as evidence of your incompetence. This makes it easier to admit them and to move on. Similarly, with a growth mindset, you are more likely to focus on others' strengths and see them as role models you can learn from and be inspired by, rather than as rivals who are ready to beat you. Open-mindedness and teachability, as we have previously mentioned, are hallmarks of humbitious leaders.

"Humble people believe they can be[come] better people than they currently are," wrote Brad Owens in his groundbreaking dissertation. Basing his ideas on thirty interviews with seventeen leaders, he suggested that when you believe your abilities can grow through hard work and perseverance, you are more likely to see yourself more accurately, to view others more positively, and to be open to new information. However, when you see your abilities as fixed, you tend to focus on what is easy for you rather than on pursuing tasks that can help you stretch and grow, and you tend to engage in self-enhancing behaviors. Having a growth mindset, then, significantly predisposes you to be more humble.

Views and Beliefs

Somewhat related to the concept of mindset is the amount of self-esteem that a leader has. Self-esteem is your confidence in your own worth and abilities, and low self-esteem is related to having insecurities. When you have insecurities, you are afraid to accept and show your weaknesses to others. In order to value others' strengths and embrace your weaknesses, you need to start from a place of safety. This connection between self-esteem and humility has been documented in several empirical studies. When you act in humble ways, you are exposing the most vulnerable parts of yourself. If you don't have the necessary self-confidence to handle the implications of your vulnerabilities, you will have a hard time showing your humility.

Other self-beliefs are also closely related to humility. Psychological analyses show that some people tend to have an individual identity orientation, where they perceive themselves as independent, self-focused, and self-interested. Others have a relational identity: they define themselves in terms of their role relationships with others. If you have this latter type of identity, you tend to sacrifice personal benefits for the good of others, you are inclined to uphold your commitments, and you are likely to value deep connections with others. Studies have revealed that leaders with relational identity were also more likely to be seen as humble leaders by their team members.

Another possible contributor to a leader's humility is their degree of religiosity or morality. As we discussed in Chapter 1, humility has deep roots in the major religions and philosophies of morality. Julie Exline and Anne Geyer from Case Western Reserve University found, based on a survey of undergraduate students, that religious individuals viewed humility more favorably and that humble students were more likely to be religious. I recently interviewed Deneese Jones, the vice president of academic affairs at Trinity University, a truly humble and caring leader who has led several institutions to outstanding performance over the course of her career. When I asked her about the origins of her humble style, she attributed it mainly to her beliefs: "My faith plays a huge role in that. But I'm not talking about religion, I'm talking about God calling me to do this work; he gave me the skills and talents."

Certain Death and Role Models

We can conclude from the previous section that the mindset and beliefs you have about yourself and your relations with others can shape the degree of your humility. What factors, then, determine how you acquire these mindsets and beliefs in the first place?

When I was in first grade, I had an amazingly kind teacher who made learning fun and who made every child feel like they could reach for the stars. If we couldn't read a tough word or if we messed up a drawing, she gave us words of encouragement and pushed us to do better. My parents modeled similar traits every day. My father is kind and fun. My mother is strong and caring. Together, they combined humility and ambition. While they were both leaders in their respective jobs (my father was a bank executive, my mother was a director at a nonprofit organization), it was at home where they best demonstrated their humbitious approach: they treated my brother and me with care and love while setting clear expectations. They never made a big deal out of a good grade and never yelled at us for a bad grade—it was always about whether we were putting in enough effort and trying as hard as we could. They emphasized that we were unique and special, but no better than anyone else. I believe that these lessons set me on the right path to start developing my humility at an early age (the irony of bragging about my own humility is not lost on me here). In addition to some other experiences early in my life, my first-grade teacher and my parents laid the foundation for me to become an adult who is generally comfortable with who he is and who believes he can, within reason, do anything he sets his mind to (including writing a book like this one).

As we saw in Stacey Taylor's experience, the type of family experiences and the style of upbringing that a person undergoes can have a key effect on the type of leader they turn out to be. When you have safe attachments, have humbitious parents and teachers, and receive reality-based feedback, you are more likely to develop your own humility over time. However, as Exline and Geyer explain, if you experience an upbringing with "extreme emphasis on performance, appearance ... or other external sources of self-evaluations" and "inaccurate, excessive praise or criticism," you are more likely to drift away from humility. The type of situations that you go through early on in life, then, can plant the seeds of humility. Sometimes, though, it could be later life experiences that open your eyes and redirect you to the path of humility.

Sometimes you may have the potential to become humble, but you forget it or fail to develop it. When triggered by a specific person or event, you might then begin to self-reflect and engage in conscious personal development. Your humility starts to be nurtured and you begin to progress towards that leadership style. Darwin Smith, another Good-to-Great leader, learned that he had throat cancer around the same time he got the top job at Kimberly-Clark. The doctors told him he had one year to live, at most. He underwent radiation treatment and, against all odds, regained his health. This experience forced him to reflect on his personal values and leadership, and he went on to serve as a very successful CEO for twenty years. At his retirement, when asked about the secret of his success, he said, "I never stopped becoming qualified for the job."

Naturally, not everyone needs to be diagnosed with cancer, or to escape from certain death, in order to start this kind of transformation. Sometimes, receiving critical feedback can force you to course-correct. For example, one of the leaders interviewed by Brad Owens told this remarkable story about his previous boss: "I left one of my last companies because of this leader's arrogance, his flat out arrogance. [He was] taking ideas from somebody like myself and coining them as his own and sending that to upper management... But I just had a conversation with a couple of my previous co-workers a short while ago and their comment about him was 'he's changed'... They said he'd received some tongue lashings from upper management and it made him take a real step back. They said he doesn't micromanage nearly as much. So ... I think he has learned to be humble."

Other times, you may encounter a humble coach, mentor, or boss who inspires you to change your ways. For example, a mentor may be comfortable sharing their strengths and weaknesses with you, and may encourage you to self-reflect and seek feedback. These types of people can have a lasting influence on your leadership style: they remain there, in the back of your mind, long after you have left the organization. In the first month of my doctoral studies at the University of Minnesota, I met a highly intelligent and extremely generous professor named Jim Begun. Jim had fluffy white hair, a big smile, and a dry sense of humor. At that time, I was interested in organizational theory and behavior but my department did not offer such a course. Jim, a known expert on the topic, kindly offered to design and offer a customized independent study course for me. Over the course of the semester, we met one-on-one in his office as well as in the cafeteria and had fascinating discussions on different theoretical and practical perspectives.

In these meetings, Jim challenged me to stretch out of my comfort zone and to look at issues from new perspectives, while showing exceptional interest in my learning and development. This independent study course was the beginning of a long-term professional relationship that I continue to have and treasure with him. In the following semesters, he asked me to work as his teaching assistant and his research assistant. Co-teaching with Jim was one of the best learning experiences in my career. Rather than delegating typical "TA duties" to me, such as grading papers and holding office hours, he went out of his way to involve me in developing course sessions and gave me ample opportunities to teach and interact with graduate students in order to develop and refine my teaching skills. After each class session, he would sit down with me and give me honest feedback about my strengths and my areas for improvement. The energy and care that I observed him putting into the design and execution of his lectures was extraordinary and has served as the benchmark I have tried to work towards for the rest of my career. To this day, when I encounter any situation in my professional life, I ask myself, "What would Jim do?" and try to emulate his humble and generous approach.

Mentors like Jim can shape your understanding of what a leader should look like and how to go about fulfilling your own roles. Another leader interviewed by Owens echoes these sentiments: "I actually had a really, really strong leader. I didn't realize how strong he was until long after I left the company... He was extremely talented at getting other people to go where he needed and checking the right people in the right places that all went under him. So as I'm picturing him, now I get it. Trying to develop more humility has allowed me to understand now that that was the way he was and I can absolutely take some of those techniques that he did so well and use them in my day to day work."

Getting the Soldiers over the Hill

In the previous chapter, we discussed the ample evidence showing that humility enables leaders to achieve high performance for themselves, their teams, and their organizations. However, it would be impractical, if not outright naïve, to declare that humility is the only leadership approach in all types of organizations and for all situations. There are certainly some situations where the value of humility can be limited, or where humble leaders may actually be *less* effective than non-humble ones.

As a humbitious leader, you listen to your followers and show appreciation towards them. You invest your time in growing and developing your team members by giving them advice, opening doors for them, and providing them with learning opportunities. However, in times of extreme threats, when the status quo of the organization is severely disrupted, the last thing employees need is for you to be open-minded and vulnerable. For example, if you are the CEO of a large hospital on the Florida coast preparing for a Category 5 hurricane and having to arrange for the transfer of hundreds of patients and for protecting the safety of your employees, you don't need to show humility right then; there is little room at that moment for discussion, learning, and development. What you need is to make swift decisions to assign responsibilities and coordinate activities that serve to re-stabilize the situation and dissipate people's fears and insecurities. "When you need to get your soldiers over the hill, it is not a time to get opinions," a wise leader once declared. This possibly explains why decisive, take-charge types of leaders such as Winston Churchill were extremely successful during times of war, and why their leadership style was viewed as incompatible with more peaceful times requiring humility, consensus, and collaboration.

Similarly, when you face an internal or external threat in the form of aggressive individuals or groups, your humility may not be the best weapon for fighting those threats. A couple of years ago, I got invited to speak at Hôtel-Dieu Grace Healthcare in Windsor, Ontario. During my short visit, I had the chance to meet several high-performing leaders, and none of them exemplified humbitious leadership more than the CEO of the organization, Janice Kaffer. After discussing how her approach has helped her achieve individual and organizational success, I asked Janice if she had ever encountered a situation where her humble approach did not work. "Yes. We had a conflict once," she said. "My humility was interpreted as a weakness." I asked Janice how she dealt with the situation: Did she change her style or did she accept that she couldn't win in this situation? "Actually, I went with a third option," she explained. "I had a colleague who is strong and more forceful, so I brought them with me to the meetings. And we resolved the situation in our favor." While the main argument of this book is that humbitious leaders are more effective than non-humbitious ones, there are certainly situations where a leader has to admit that their style may not work and that they need to adopt a different one or call on other leaders in the organization whose style can complement theirs. Due in large part to her humility, Janice had the emotional intelligence and self-awareness to recognize this and to be agile enough to change her style and bring in the help needed to complement her abilities, in order to achieve the desired goal for the organization.

"I Feel like I Am Disappearing"

As a leader, it is very possible that you have worked in organizations where senior leaders behave in authoritarian, self-serving ways. These types of organizations have cultures that are built on competition and rivalry, rather than on learning and collaboration. In these settings, humility may not be appreciated or even validated. As a humble leader, if you find yourself working in these organizations, it becomes very hard for you to stay authentic to your values and achieve success. Deneese Jones, whom we met earlier, can relate to these situations: "It becomes really problematic if you are humble and serving and someone who has authority over you does not appreciate it. It happened to me before in my career; you become marginalized; it is crushing, you feel invisible." So, I asked her, how do you deal with the situation? "I don't have a good answer for that. I feel like I am disappearing. I just remove myself; I have the strength to say 'no, this is not for me.'" In dealing with conditions like this, you have to decide if it is worth it for you to endure this culture for the sake of financial security or career development, or if it would be better for your wellbeing to leave the organization all together.

Is it possible that some followers prefer a non-humble style from their leaders over a more humble one? Jia Hu from Ohio State University and her colleagues set out to answer this question. They examined members of seventy-two teams working at eleven information and technology firms in China. To better understand what factors might limit the effectiveness of leader humility, they measured the power distance in every team. Team power distance is the degree to which members of the team believe that it is legitimate for the leader to have significantly more power than the members. In the study, power distance was measured using items such as, "When a performance appraisal made by the supervisor does not fit with subordinates' expectations, the employees should feel free to discuss it with the supervisor." The results showed that, as expected, in teams with lower power distance, humble leaders encouraged their team members to share information with each other. In contrast, in high power-distance teams, humble leaders did not affect team information sharing, and even negatively impacted psychological safety.

It is not hard to see that in those teams with steep hierarchies, humble behaviors may trigger negative emotional experiences among team members, where they may feel dissatisfied or frustrated with their leaders. Humble leaders are met with doubt, which results in team members feeling unsafe to take risks. The authors warn that "not everyone wants a humble leader, so you need to adapt your style to your team's expectations. However, if the people you lead do expect humility, demonstrating it can benefit team creativity and success." Some organizations or teams have a strong adherence to hierarchy and rules. In this environment of authority and chain of command, leaders do not feel particularly encouraged to admit their mistakes in public or to acknowledge others' contributions.

Danny Anderson, president of Trinity University and a humbitious leader himself, has encountered similar power dynamics in his career. So often, when he started a new position or came to a new organization, he found that some of his new team members were used to working for authoritarians and were expecting the same from him. They wanted a patriarch, were expecting heads to roll, and were disappointed by his humble leadership approach. "But then, some of them you will win over with your strength and persistence. They see that you can move mountains one inch at a time," he explained. "But others, because of the baggage that they have, the resentment from the past, they are never able to see beyond those feelings to see you and your impact." In dealing with these types of followers, the humble leader may wish to temporarily modify their style if they are to get that group motivated and on board.

Nicole (not her real name) is a thirty-two-year-old executive who was recently promoted to the position of COO of a large hospital in a booming metropolitan area. She has eighteen middle managers who report to her—directors of dietary, food services, pharmacy, radiology, and so on. Most of these directors are older men who have been in their positions for a long time. As one of them half-jokingly told her, "I came to this hospital when you were still in diapers!" Nicole's leadership style is open, collaborative, and appreciative. As she told me when I worked with her, "I am not your typical executive; I don't look like the other executives. Sometimes I wonder: Why have they thought I can do this job? And I think it's because of my ability to build trust: I am accountable, I build relationships with people. I set expectations, I am honest, and I give feedback from a place of love and care."

Most of the directors who work for her come from the old-fashioned school of command and control. They make unilateral decisions and announce them to their staff with little to no input. So, how will this discrepancy between Nicole and her followers affect her performance as a leader?

The evidence shows that not only do employees' expectations of a leader have an impact on the effectiveness of that leader, but so do the traits and predispositions of the employees themselves. The level of employee humility can play a key role in the success or failure of a humbitious leader. A study conducted among a large bank group, for example, showed that when employee humility was lower than leader humility, the employees felt irritated, nervous, and distressed about their supervisor. This, in turn, resulted in them being more likely to engage in counterproductive work behaviors, such as wasting the company's materials and supplies, and less likely to help co-workers with heavy workloads. Congruence between leaders and followers is an important but often neglected dynamic in teams and organizations. The research is clear that when there is a mismatch between your humility level and your employees' humility levels, they are more likely to have negative feelings towards you and to behave in less effective ways. As a leader, you need to be cognizant of the humility of your team, and to show more confidence when you sense that humility is not appreciated. Eventually, if you truly believe that humility is the best way to lead, you may want to consider replacing those team members who don't align with your style and the culture you are aspiring to create.

In addition to these insights on leader and follower beliefs and traits, other studies have shown that demographic differences can play a role in the effectiveness of humility. Humble leadership resulted in followers' increased willingness to internalize their leader's attributes and to achieve better quality and quantity of work output, but only when the leader and followers were of similar age and gender. The authors noted that "although expressing humility could be an effective leadership style, we caution leaders that showing humility may not bring the expected benefit in followers, particularly when followers are demographically dissimilar from leaders." It makes sense that a humble young female leader, like Nicole, can better relate to young female team members. She is more likely to be effective in influencing her team members than if they were older males, for example. I am not advocating for Nicole to completely abandon her humble leadership for the sake of appeasing her directors. However, she would be wise to adjust her style depending on the situation to make sure she is not perceived as weak or lacking in assertiveness. Over time, as her competence and knowledge become more accepted, she could feel more comfortable showing more of her true humble self.

What Next?

We have seen that there are various factors that may predispose a leader to become more humble: childhood experiences, religiousness or morality, role models, and significant life events. And we are faced with the fact that, in some situations, humility can be less effective or even counterproductive, such as in crisis situations with immediate threats or organizational cultures that emphasize authority and rivalry. Given this, here are some action items for your own development:

- Adopt a growth mindset and believe that your qualities can be cultivated through effort.

- Seek mentors who challenge you and genuinely care for you.

- Recognize situations and cultures where humbitiousness may not be the right approach and adjust accordingly.

- Surround yourself with leaders who have different strengths that can complement your weaknesses.

In the next part, we will switch to humble leadership in relation to the self, beginning with a deep dive into self-awareness.

two

Humble Leadership in Relation to the Self

4

Self-Awareness

The first product of self-knowledge is humility.
FLANNERY O'CONNOR

"I Don't See It"

"Nuh-uh, I don't believe it, man. I don't see it." Travis Kalanick, the young co-founder, pushed at his recently hired president, Jeff Jones, and the rest of the Uber executive team. His lack of self-awareness had never been more apparent than at this moment.

The setting was a conference room at the Le Méridien hotel in downtown San Francisco in February 2017. Jones, who was brought in a few months earlier to fix Uber's public perception problem, had called for the meeting to discuss the results of a survey he had commissioned. He had wanted to know how people viewed Uber, and, most importantly, how they viewed Kalanick. Knowing that the results were sensitive, Jones had invited the executive team but had specifically asked Kalanick not to attend the meeting.

The morning started without Kalanick as Jones shared the results. He explained to the team that the public loved Uber as a service and enjoyed using it. However, people said they hated Travis Kalanick. It was clear to the executives that Uber didn't have an *image problem*. It had a *Travis problem*. After much deliberation, the executives wrote in bold black ink on a large piece of paper what they believed people thought when they thought of Uber: "A bunch of young bro bullies that have achieved ridiculous success."

Meanwhile, Kalanick was feeling antsy and left out. He texted Jones to tell him he was on his way to the meeting. By the time he arrived, the team had the large piece of paper already hanging in the middle of the room. As he came in, Kalanick stared at the writing on the paper. But with the little self-awareness that he had, he couldn't accept what the public was saying. He didn't believe it. He just couldn't see how *he* was the problem. Jones and the executives, armed with the data, fought back.

And then, in the middle of this heated discussion, one of the executives got a phone call and stepped out of the room to answer it. Moments later, she signaled to another executive to come out. Something seriously wrong had happened. Before too long, Jones, Kalanick, and the other executives were huddled in the hallway around a laptop, watching a video. The footage, shot from inside an Uber car, showed Travis Kalanick and a couple of women in the back seat, with a driver in the front.

A few minutes into the video, as Kalanick and his companions are getting ready to leave the car, the driver starts talking to him and says that he knows who he is. The conversation heats up and the driver questions Kalanick on why Uber had dropped its prices and slashed its drivers' incomes.

"I lost $97,000 because of you," the driver exclaims. "I'm bankrupt because of you. You keep changing every day."

"Hold on a second! What have I changed...?" replies Kalanick.

"You dropped everything!" the driver pushes.

As he begins to make his was out of the car, Kalanick shouts: "Bullshit. You know what? Some people don't like to take responsibility for their own shit!" He then waves his finger at the driver: "They blame everything in their life on somebody else. Good luck!"

In the hallway, the executives were stunned. Kalanick was on his knees, slowly whispering to himself: "This is bad. This is really bad." At a later meeting that afternoon, Kalanick couldn't stop repeating over and over: "I'm a terrible person. I'm a terrible person. I'm a terrible person." His earlier defiance was now replaced by total surrender. But the board had had enough. They voted to fire him.

What can you learn from the case of Travis Kalanick? No matter how fast the growth or how good the product, a poisonous leadership style that lacks self-awareness will always result in a toxic organizational culture—one that will lead to backfire. Since the founding of Uber, Kalanick's approach was to win at all costs, ignore laws, and compete to humiliate other companies. He rarely listened to others, promoted a male chauvinist "bro-culture," and tastelessly referred to his company as "boob-er" because it allowed him to attract women. He had set the tone for a culture where groping female co-workers at company retreats, shouting homophobic slurs at subordinates during meetings, and threatening to beat underperforming employees with baseball bats had become the norm.

While Uber's product was widely loved, Kalanick's narcissistic personality impacted the brand so negatively that the company had lost $20 billion in its market valuation by the time of his exit. Yes, self-centered jerks can create great start-ups and lead them to unprecedented growth. But long-term success can't be achieved unless there are humble, self-aware leaders at the top. It is tempting to think that Kalanick's apologies and promises after the numerous crises his actions created were based on deep self-insights and honest feedback. The more likely truth is that they were publicity statements put out by someone who rarely reflected on his own leadership and hardly listened to others. As the organizational psychologist and self-awareness expert Tasha Eurich rightly pointed out, "Like so many rock-star entrepreneurs who shoot to success only to fall from grace, Kalanick has demonstrated a lack of the most critical (yet least understood) skill in the business world: self-awareness." The first step in gaining an understanding of yourself is to build self-awareness. Let us then focus on the importance of self-awareness for humbitious leaders and their long-term success.

Meformers

First, what is self-awareness? You probably know someone who lacks self-awareness, but you might find it hard to define what self-awareness really is. In her remarkable book *Insight*, Eurich explains that "self-awareness is the will and skill to understand yourself and how others see you." Based on extensive research involving more than 5,000 participants, she found that while 95 percent of people believe they are self-aware, only 10 to 15 percent are actually self-aware. What this means, Eurich joked in her TEDx talk, is that on a good day, most of us are lying to ourselves about how we are lying to ourselves.

To better understand the components of self-awareness, she tracked people to identify what made some improve their self-awareness over time—a rare occurrence. The research revealed that self-awareness has an internal and an extern. component. Internally, self-awareness is about understand ing our own values, passions, aspirations, fit, patterns, reactions, and impact on others. Values, as we will see in the next chapter, are our non-negotiables. Passions are what we love to do, and aspirations are what we want to achieve and experience. Fit refers to the type of environment we need to be happy and engaged; patterns are our consistent ways of thinking, feeling, and behaving, as well as our strengths and weaknesses (which relate to personality and emotional intel-ligence); while reactions are the thoughts and feelings that reveal our true capabilities. Finally, impact is the effect we believe we have on others. People who increase their inter-nal self-awareness typically do so by introspecting in ways that are objective and future-focused. This type of introspec-tion empowers better decisions and actions. As Peter Drucker, the father of management, said, "Follow effective action with quiet reflection. From the quiet reflection will come even more effective action."

Externally, self-awareness requires an understanding of how others view us, and the best way to gain that is to ask for feedback and to listen to it, which we will cover in depth in a few pages. Interestingly, the research shows there is no relationship between internal and external self-awareness: a leader can have one and not the other. An "introspector," in Eurich's terms, is someone who has high internal and low external self-awareness, whereas a "pleaser" has high external and low internal self-awareness. Ideally, you want to have both in order to be truly self-aware and achieve high performance.

Research in the last thirty years has documented the vital benefits of self-awareness for employees, and for all people in general. Self-aware individuals tend to make better decisions, have better relations with others, are able to take the perspective of others, have more self-control, are more creative, and have higher self-esteem than those who lack self-awareness. Similarly, employees with high self-awareness typically report healthier wellbeing, communicate better with their colleagues, and have higher confidence than others.

However, it is especially in the domain of leadership where self-awareness provides the clearest advantages. For example, an in-depth study of leaders in the United Kingdom showed that those who were more successful in driving major organizational changes demonstrated superior self-awareness: they continuously reflected on their own behaviors; they noticed their own impulses and struggles and reflected on what they could have done differently; and, most importantly, they regularly sought feedback from others. Similarly, a study of 9,000 leader self-assessments and their corresponding 360-degree feedback reports showed that self-aware leaders were one-sixth as likely to be at risk of derailment as non-self-aware ones. Other studies have shown strong relationships between leader self-awareness and their followers' satisfaction and productivity; their own performance and effectiveness as leaders; and their organizations' outcomes.

How does self-awareness relate directly to humility? As we discussed before, humility is about having an accurate view of yourself: understanding your talents and accomplishments while accepting your imperfections and shortcomings. As a humbitious leader, you become aware of your own strengths and weaknesses based on disciplined self-reflection and honest feedback from others. "Because it means appreciating our weaknesses and keeping our successes in perspective, humility is a key ingredient of self-awareness," notes Eurich.

This important connection is well supported by research. Self-aware individuals tend to see the self as a cause of success, which leads to positive feelings of healthy self-esteem. Their self-awareness enables true confidence, but not arrogance. Along the same line, self-aware leaders neither overestimate nor underestimate their own leadership strengths—they tend to rate themselves similarly to how others rate them. The previously mentioned U.K. study uncovered that self-aware leaders were successful change agents because they avoided falling into the traps of their egos: they didn't get caught in their own needs and agendas but rather tried to serve an organizational purpose beyond themselves.

Nowadays, self-focus is a major obstacle for individuals and leaders in gaining self-awareness. For example, the majority of people use social media to make posts that tell others about their own days and lives. These types of people can be referred to as self-absorbed *Meformers*. But a small minority of people (around 20 percent) are self-aware *Informers*. They use social media to post non-self-related articles and quotes that inform, amuse, or inspire others. Recent research shows that Informers tend to have richer interactions and happier lives than Meformers. Tasha Eurich explained to me that the same labels can apply to leaders: "Humble leaders are Informers rather than Meformers; hold an accurate, but not overly critical, view of their abilities; and trust the contributions and expertise of others. For all of these reasons, not only are they more self-aware, but they have more engaged teams who get better results."

Others Know Us Better

We have so far discussed the internal and external components of self-awareness and its benefits for people and leaders. A key method for you to gain external self-awareness, as we briefly mentioned, is to seek feedback from others. So let's focus on the various ways that you can obtain productive feedback, both formally and informally.

So, why can't you just rely on your own understanding of yourself, and why is it important to ask others for their perceptions of you? Psychological research has shown that blind spots—those parts of our personality that we can't see but that others clearly see—are substantial. There are several factors that cause these misperceptions. Sometimes, your blind spots are simply due to a lack of information about yourself. You may have a habit of frowning when listening intently, for example, which makes you appear intimidating to your team members. After a colleague or brave subordinate delicately brings this to your attention, you start making an effort to have an authentic smile when people talk to you. Another reason for blind spots is having too much information about yourself, so that you are unable to see the forest for the trees. For example, you can think of many times when you have acted in a humble way with others, but also of times when you acted in a self-centered way. As a result, you may be unable to mentally aggregate whether you are generally humble or not.

The last reason for blind spots is not as innocent as the first two: your constant motivation to maintain and enhance your self-worth can have a strong influence on your self-perception. What this means is that, in order to maintain a positive view of yourself, you may convince yourself that you are always acting in the best interest of others, while, in reality, most of your actions are driven by self-centered motives. You tell yourself a story about being a servant leader, for example, and you end up believing that story.

In a thoughtfully designed study, Simine Vazire and Erika Carlson from Washington University in St. Louis examined these types of blind spots by comparing self and friend ratings of personality to how people behaved in videotaped laboratory exercises and how they performed on intelligence and creativity tests. For internal, neutral traits such as anxiety and self-esteem, self-rating was more accurate than friend ratings. However, on evaluative traits such as intelligence and creativity, friend ratings were actually closer to the truth than self-rating, leading the researchers to conclude that others know a lot about us that we don't know, and that the best way to tap into others' knowledge is to ask for direct and honest feedback. Most organizations assume that annual performance evaluations allow supervisors to provide this type of feedback to their direct reports, but anyone who has been through one of these sessions knows that they don't always work as well as they should.

The identification of blind spots is a common theme in my work as an executive coach. One case that is still fresh in my mind is that of Dr. Kim (not her real name), a cardiology division chief at a large academic medical center. When her boss, the dean of the school of medicine, called me to discuss the coaching engagement, he explained that Dr. Kim was a high-performing leader and was internationally recognized for her cutting-edge research. However, he said, she was very difficult to work with. She had been with the organization less than a year, but had already generated some ill feelings at various levels of the institution, and many viewed her as critical and entitled. "On a personal level, she is very charming, a good person. She just lacks the insight on how her actions are perceived by others," the dean clarified.

After the initial kick-off, we conducted a 360-feedback survey and sought the input of several of her superiors, colleagues, and direct reports. I also asked her to evaluate herself on the same leadership components that are in the survey.

The results showed that the dean was correct in his assessment: Dr. Kim had some glaring blind spots. On most questions, she gave herself higher ratings than others did. One respondent commented, "She is not aware that she can come across to subordinates as being a bit aloof." Another added, "She calls attention to herself on successes. Seems oblivious to how others in her group feel about her. Is viewed as self-centered." Despite initial feelings of shock and disbelief, Dr. Kim finally understood that if she wanted to become a more effective leader, she needed to pay more attention to the impact of her actions on others and how she is perceived by them. After several honest and hard conversations, we put together a detailed plan to address her blind spots, and, in the process, to improve her self-awareness and humility. With this plan in hand, she was on her way to becoming a more humbitious leader.

360 and More

The 360-degree feedback survey is one of the most prevalent tools used in leadership development. The research shows that leaders who receive unfavorable feedback or who initially overrate themselves, like Dr. Kim, tend to improve more than others, which supports the idea that feedback creates new self-awareness and a perceived need for change. While some organizations hire executive coaches to do the survey for their leaders and to walk them through the results, many others conduct the 360 surveys internally for all of their executives across the board. Problems can arise in the latter case, though, when organizations conduct their own surveys but provide no support for the executives in interpreting the results.

Often, you are given your reports and left to decipher the findings on your own. This approach allows you to get only 25 percent of the benefit of the feedback. To get the other 75 percent, executive coach Jennifer Porter suggests additional steps, starting with a chance to reflect on your results with a trusted partner. If it is not possible to hire an executive coach, then a non-judgmental peer or a mentor from outside the organization can help you think through important questions that inform self-awareness. These questions may include:

- What exactly did the feedback report tell me?

- How open am I to accepting the data as evidence of others' experiences with me?

- What impact am I having on others?

- How does that compare to the impact I want to have?

These questions will generate sober reflections, and based on that, you can draft a development plan. You are then encouraged to schedule 1:1 meetings with the respondents who provided the feedback. The goal of these meetings is not to debate or question the results, but rather to thank the respondents, ask specific questions, request examples on unclear scores and comments, and share the draft improvement plan. The insights obtained in these meetings can help you revise the plan and start implementing it by taking actions to improve.

We should explain that while comparing their own to other's ratings can provide important insights about a leader's self-awareness, researchers have also suggested some additional methods. Scott Taylor, an expert on leader self-awareness with Babson College, proposes that asking people to predict how others see a leader and then comparing that to how others *actually* see that leader can also be an accurate measure of self-awareness. He calls this measure the "prediction-other" rating. If you are a leader with high external self-awareness, you are able to accurately read the emotions, thoughts, and preferences of others, as well as your influence on them. You can anticipate how others experience your behavior, and are able to accurately assess what your superiors, colleagues, or direct reports feel as well as how you come across to them and affect them. In one paper, Taylor and his team measured leaders' assessment of their own competencies and how they predicted others would rate them on these same competencies. The findings showed that "prediction-other" rating was a better explainer of leader effectiveness than "self-other" rating. This suggests that leaders are more effective when they are more attuned to how their direct reports perceive them on leadership competencies, rather than when their self-perception is just the same as their direct reports'.

Annual performance evaluations and 360 feedback are not the only way to obtain and give feedback. Progressive organizations like Netflix, for example, have put in place other mechanisms that allow employees to practice radical honesty with each other, thus improving everyone's awareness of the perceptions that others have of them. One of the practices that Netflix (and many other organizations) have implemented is a system called "Start, Stop, Continue," where people can tell each other what they should start doing, stop doing, and continue doing, in terms of specific behaviors. They also created a "feedback day" where engineers and executives can give each other direct, face-to-face feedback. While most companies use anonymous feedback, Netflix believes that such surveys are a waste of time. "If you don't know who is giving you feedback, how can you put their comments into the context of the work they're doing, who their manager is, and what kind of employee they are?" notes Patty McCord, a former Netflix chief talent officer. While these ideas may sound a bit extreme for many organizations, they provide new ways of experimenting with feedback that is valuable and honest, thus resulting in improved self-awareness and humility.

Loving Critics and Feed*forward*

If you are fortunate to work for a boss who has your best interests at heart, make sure to listen when they give you honest and direct feedback on how you are coming across. Since most bosses are not that way, you need to be intentional about initiating the feedback-seeking process yourself. In fact, seeking feedback and asking for input is one of the most important behaviors you can engage in. Research conducted by Jack Zenger and Joe Folkman reveals that top-ranked leaders (those at or higher than the 83rd percentile in effectiveness) are also in the top percentile in asking for feedback.

Some leaders assume that seeking feedback makes them look weak or needy, but nothing could be further from the truth. It actually takes a lot of courage and strength to ask for feedback. And once you get in the habit of asking, you will continue to receive feedback from others throughout your career because people will come to perceive you as open and willing to change. Folkman recently explained to me that leaders who believe they have a fixed ability to improve cannot afford to be humble. Asking for feedback, in their minds, makes them look pathetic, so they resist it and become defensive. However, confident leaders who believe in their own ability to change are humble enough to ask for feedback and accept it.

Other than improving self-awareness, there are more important benefits to asking for feedback. For one, when you ask others for their input rather than waiting for them to give you unsolicited feedback, you are less likely to be defensive, and more likely to listen carefully and accept the remarks. Moreover, when people are asked for feedback, they are more likely to take the time to give an honest and productive perspective, rather than providing general empty statements.

How should you go about the process of asking for informal feedback from others? The first step is to identify a small group of people who have your best interests in mind and are willing to tell you the truth—what experts call "loving critics." John Hornbeak, a retired healthcare executive, once told me that when he became CEO of the Methodist Healthcare System in San Antonio, he asked one of his vice presidents to act as his appointed critic, especially in meetings. After an especially heated meeting, the vice president would take John aside and say, "Today you didn't listen well," or, "In this meeting you were a bit rude." The vice president felt comfortable providing this type of feedback to his boss because John encouraged and rewarded honesty and never became defensive after hearing such input. When selecting loving critics, it is important to pick people who have repeated exposure to you and to the behaviors that you are seeking feedback on, and to have someone who understands what success looks like.

Once you've identified who to talk to, a good approach is to ask for specific feedback on particular situations, instead of asking a blanket question such as, "What feedback do you have for me?" For example, after a meeting, you can approach a trusted colleague and ask, "How did I come across in this meeting?" or, "What specific improvements can I make on my presentation?" Similarly, you can seek specific input about worrisome patterns that you may have noticed in yourself, such as, "How often do you notice me interrupting people in meetings?" You can also inquire about the personal impact of your actions by asking, "How did it feel to you when I said that in the meeting?" Alternatively, you can seek specific recommendations related to dealing with other people, like, "What can I do to improve my relationship with Jose?"

In these interactions, it is helpful to ask for both positive and negative data, because positive input can alert you to "bright spots" or hidden strengths that relate to behaviors that you should continue doing. It is also crucial to listen carefully, never defend your actions or debate the other person, and demonstrate gratitude to them. After collecting enough input, spend some time reflecting and evaluating on what to consider, what to disregard, and what requires deeper thinking. Based on that, make a plan to take action and share periodic updates on your progress with the people who have helped obtain the insights.

Sometimes, using different words when seeking input can allow us to get better insights from others. In one research study, participants who were asked for "advice" suggested 34 percent more areas for improvement and 56 percent more ways to improve than those who were asked for "feedback." For many, the term feedback has a negative connotation that invokes evaluation and judgment, and this results in less actionable input. "Feedback is screechy and makes us want to put our hands over our ears," notes Kim Scott, a former

Google executive. Advice, or guidance, on the other hand, is more future-oriented and focuses on opportunities to improve.

This notion is similar to the difference between feedback and feed*forward*, a term used by world-renowned executive coach Marshall Goldsmith. After leaders have received feedback about their strengths, weaknesses, and others' perceptions of them, it is time for them to turn their attention from past behaviors to future ones by using feedforward. Goldsmith introduced this concept in his coaching practices because he was frustrated with traditional feedback mechanisms, which forced leaders to relive the past over and over again. He wanted feedback that went in the other direction, an approach that focuses on ideas that leaders can practice in the future. "If feedback is past tense, then feedforward is future perfect," he explains in his book *What Got You Here Won't Get You There*.

Feedforward starts after you have identified your areas for improvement, based on self-reflection and input from others. You begin by picking one specific behavior change that will have a significant positive impact on your effectiveness as a leader. For example, you may decide that you want to become a better listener. You then identify a number of people who can help you improve on this behavior, such as your supervisor, a trusted colleague, an insightful direct report, or even your spouse, friend, or sibling. You then approach each person face-to-face and declare: "I want to be a better listener. Would you suggest two ideas that I can implement in the future that will help me become a better listener?" As the person gives you their ideas, you listen carefully and never answer in a judging or defensive way. You just thank them, then move on to repeat the process with someone else. As you collect a satisfactory number of suggestions, you decide which comments you will consider and which you will not. The main reason feedforward works so well is that, like most high performers, you don't like to hear criticisms, but you love getting ideas for the future and working on implementing them. Feedforward, by design, is not threatening and is compatible with our inherent drive to improve ourselves.

Self-Distancing

Self-reflection and introspection, as we will see in the next chapter, require you to think deeply about yourself. Similarly, when you receive feedback or feedforward from others, you need to dedicate time and effort to thinking hard about what they told you and how you can make changes. However, sometimes the problem is in your thinking itself; it is your own thoughts that may be blocking your self-awareness or contributing to your arrogance. In that case, what is needed is not *more* thinking, but rather separating yourself from your thoughts so you can see them more clearly. And this is where mindfulness comes in.

Of the numerous buzzwords that have made their way into the leadership lexicon in the last few years, "mindfulness" must rank at the top of the list. Leadership seminars, articles, and books claim that if we just learn to be more mindful leaders, we can achieve anything. While most of these claims are hyped up and don't have much evidence behind them, the truth is that mindfulness, when practiced in the right way, can be a key path to better self-awareness and humility.

What is mindfulness in the context of leadership, you may ask? It is paying attention, in the present time, with a clear, calm, and focused mind. When most people think about mindfulness, the image of a monk in a red robe sitting in a cave for days, months, or years comes to mind. And while that is definitely one way to attain mindfulness, it is not the only way. You do not need to sit on a mat for hours or even go to a two-week retreat to become a more mindful leader. It is actually far simpler than that.

Mindfulness is about noticing your behavior while it is happening. It is about focusing on one task at a time, while being aware of what is happening around you to make sure that you are paying attention to important distractions and ignoring unimportant ones. One of the most important benefits of mindfulness is that it can improve your self-awareness by pushing you to distance yourself from your own inaccurate thoughts, a practice called *self-distancing*. So often, our thoughts are just expressions of our ego talking to us: "I am better than her," "I am smarter than him," "They hate me because I am so good," and so on. But you should stop believing everything you think, says leadership consultant Cy Wakeman in her insightful book *No Ego*. You are not your thoughts, and you don't need to believe them all the time.

That is why sometimes it is important to listen to your thoughts and record them—so that you can separate yourself from them. When you find yourself marred with arrogant, self-centered thoughts, one way you can practice self-distancing is by pretending that you are talking to another person, such as a friend or loved one. Another approach is to journal in the third person. Instead of writing, "Today I experienced this during the weekly meeting," you can write, "Today, he experienced this during the weekly meeting." While initially awkward, this separation allows you to build self-awareness and to have more insight by clearing the way for you to zoom out of your own self.

In addition to pretending that you are talking to someone else or journaling in the third person, practicing mindfulness meditation can allow you to create space between your thoughts and yourself. If you had told me ten years ago that I would be writing about meditation and advocating for it, I would have thought you had lost your mind. For some reason, I had always convinced myself that meditation is some flaky, new-agey stuff dreamed up by people who have a lot of time on their hands. However, as I have been learning more and more about high-performing leaders and their best practices, I can't afford to ignore the evidence anymore: mindfulness meditation works!

About two years ago, I decided to try mindfulness for myself. I downloaded the Headspace app, went into my bedroom, put the headphones on, and sat on the floor to meditate. First day, nothing happened. Second day, still nothing happened. Too many thoughts, too much traffic in my head. But "you need to stick with it," said the voice in the app in a British accent. So I did, and, after a few weeks, I experienced something strange and wonderful: I started seeing my thoughts and ideas as separate from me. And that is exactly what mindfulness meditation allows you to do. With regular practice, you can build space from your thoughts. It is similar to the difference between *acting* in a high-action movie and *watching* one. In the first situation, you are completely consumed by the events going on around you. In the second, you are thoughtfully observing the events and analyzing them. The benefits of this type of separation cannot be overemphasized, especially when you are dealing with complex and uncertain situations on a daily basis. By taking yourself out of the picture, you can gain a much fuller and more holistic view of it, which yields better results.

In his best-selling book *Wherever You Go, There You Are,* Jon Kabat-Zinn explains how meditation involves watching the thinking process itself. When you watch your thoughts without being drawn into them, you can learn something profoundly liberating about thinking. This will help you become less of a prisoner to your usual thought patterns. These patterns of thinking are often very strong, but they are also typically narrow, inaccurate, self-involved, and plain wrong. Kabat-Zinn compares the process of thinking to a waterfall—a cascading of thought. When you cultivate mindfulness through meditation, you give yourself the chance to go behind your thinking, in the same way that you can sit on a rock behind a waterfall. You can observe the water, but you are not inside it.

How do you practice this type of mindfulness meditation? Start with five or ten minutes every day, sitting down with no agenda other than being fully present. You can use your breath as an anchor to direct your attention to the present moment. Inevitably, your mind will drift into various thoughts, some trivial and some important, until you finally notice that drift and bring your attention back to your breath.

Many leaders are hesitant to undertake this mindfulness journey on their own. And that is where an executive coach can play a major role. A coach can help you self-reflect, collect, and interpret feedback from others, and build in everyday mindfulness practices. Take the example of Vincent Siciliano, who was hired as CEO of New Resource Bank in California. In a short time, he managed to turn the financial outcomes around, but periodic employee engagement surveys showed that morale was extremely low and that most people in the organization thought he was the main cause of this. Siciliano was blindsided, angry, and indignant. He clearly lacked self-awareness, which made people see him as an inauthentic leader who cared only about the numbers. Fortunately, though, he was open to change and he started working with an executive coach on improving his self-awareness through mindfulness. His coach pushed him to separate himself from his defensive thoughts and to reformulate his values and what kind of leader he wanted to become. In a conversation with his executive coaches, he later admitted, "My ego had run amok. I was leading from my head and not from my heart." With this newly discovered awareness, he started to humbly work on building better connections with his team members and employees. By overcoming his ego, and by building mindfulness and self-awareness, he set himself up on the way to humble leadership and high performance.

What Next?

Seeking feedback from others is vital to building your external self-awareness and understanding how others perceive you. Some practices for you to consider are:

- Ask for a 360-degree feedback survey and work with a coach or trusted colleague to uncover your blind spots and understand the results.

- Identify loving critics and ask them for specific feedback on your past behaviors.

- Seek feed*forward* on how to change specific behaviors in the future.

- When you receive input, listen to understand, do not become defensive, and thank the other person.

· Develop a plan of action based on what you hear and periodically share it with the people who gave you the input.

This need for self-awareness requires self-reflection, which is the next step in your journey as a humbitious leader.

—— 5 ——

Self-Reflection

The unexamined life is not worth living.
SOCRATES

"Why Hasn't Anyone Told Me This Before?"

Jared (not his real name) is a young, hard-working, and intelligent leader. He is a strong operator and understands the ins and outs of the clinical and administrative units at the hospital where he works. When his boss, the hospital CEO, promoted him to the COO position, he knew that Jared had the technical knowledge to do the job, but needed to work on key aspects of his leadership style: his humility and open-mindedness. Jared had great potential and could go on to become one of the most successful leaders in the hospital system, but only if he could rein in his ego and listen more.

Jared always assumed that he was the smartest person in the room, and he made sure that everyone knew it too. He opened every meeting that he led with a long monologue about his ideas and plans, and rarely allowed anyone to push back. He seldom asked for input from others or created space for questions and discussions. Meetings were just opportunities for him to tell others what to do.

When I met with Jared for his coaching kick-off day, we spent some time getting to know each other, and then we got to his assessment reports. According to his scores, Jared's usual behavior was decisive and highly competitive. More specifically, he tended to take direct action to get things done and rarely took time to reflect before acting. He remained detached from situations involving emotional complexity and was generally objective and matter-of-fact. When communicating with others, he was direct and straightforward and did not demonstrate any sensitivity towards their opinions or feelings. In addition, Jared's emotional intelligence (EI) report revealed that his scores on self-regard and assertiveness were at least twenty-five points over the recommended "balance range," while his scores on empathy and emotional self-awareness were significantly lower.

Amazingly, this was the first time Jared had heard any of this about himself—a significant blind spot. He looked at me with disbelief and said, "Why hasn't anyone told me this before?" I explained to him that, generally, when people work with someone with high confidence and remarkable intelligence, they tend to shy away from giving direct feedback. I also explained that many aspects of his personality and EI are in fact leadership strengths: his confidence, decisiveness, and logical approach are undoubtedly what allowed him to reach the level that he was at. However, when used in excess, many of these strengths can become weaknesses: too much confidence can turn into arrogance; high decisiveness can be seen as failure to listen to opposing views; and extreme logic can become detachment from other team members. These weaknesses can be detrimental to a leader's effectiveness, especially at the highest levels. In order to get noticed early in their careers, leaders need to demonstrate independence, determination, and quick thinking. However, these very attributes may result in derailment later on.

After a long day of discussion and reflection, Jared was exhausted, but very grateful for the insights. "This is the first time in my career that I have pushed pause in order to better understand myself," he said. Reflecting on his own personality and emotional intelligence was the starting point for his growth as a humbitious leader. He has since committed to improving his humility and open-mindedness by changing the way he shows up at work every day and how he treats others on his team.

When you have a big ego, like Jared, you are conditioned to be right all the time and to win at any cost. This is the result of a lack of accurate self-reflection and a deluded view of your own abilities. Humility, on the other hand, is about having a precise view of your strengths and weaknesses. One of the starting points for this is learning about your own personality patterns and levels of EI. In my practice as a professional coach, I work with many executives like Jared who want to grow and develop as leaders. They are typically highly intelligent and overachieving individuals who want to take their performance to the next level, but they are often hindered by their lack of reflection. Self-awareness cannot be achieved without self-reflection.

Peeling the Onion

In addition to understanding your personality patterns and EI levels, if you are striving to improve your humility, you also need to go to a deeper level by reflecting and trying to understand your own values and world views. Your typical behaviors and stress reactions are visible reflections of the hidden beliefs, values, and concepts that you may or may not be aware of. The various layers in your leadership approach can be likened to peeling an onion (see the figure below). Your behaviors constitute the outer layer—how you carry out your tasks and how you interact with others on a day-to-day basis. Your personality traits, EI, knowledge, and talents occupy the middle layers. But deep in your inner conscious and subconscious layers are the world views and core values that you have developed over the course of your life. When you hold an inner thought, it gets filtered and flavored by the middle layers, and eventually manifests itself in your outward daily behaviors.

The Leader's Individual Foundation

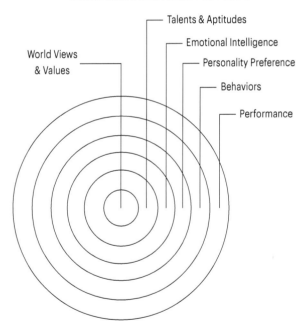

Figure 1: Adapted from Hoekstra et al., "Humility in Leadership: Abandoning the Pursuit of Unattainable Perfection."

In a fast-paced environment with overbooked schedules, back-to-back meetings, and endless interruptions and distractions, you may spend little to no energy reflecting on the inner layers of your leadership approach. With so little reflection, you end up accepting world views from others. You adopt unsound concepts that everyone around you believes in, such as "a leader should know everything or they appear weak," or "people don't need to be thanked for doing their jobs," without intentionally choosing them. The truth is that most leadership development and training programs focus on the outer layers of behaviors and actions, with little to no emphasis on deeper world views and values.

For leaders like Jared, a disciplined change in behaviors will only take them so far in their journey to improve their humility. What they also need is deliberate reflection on the values that profoundly influence their behaviors. As we started that next step in Jared's coaching process, he found this critical examination very hard. To help him acquire the required discipline, I encouraged him to draft a personal mission statement and to clarify his own values. I even got him a leather-bound leadership journal in which he could record his thoughts every day (a tool we will look at more closely in a few pages). Self-reflection and clarification of world views and values are essential for the development of humility.

One of the most significant historical examples of a leader who went to great lengths to reflect on his core values is Benjamin Franklin. At the young age of twenty-seven, Franklin started his journey towards "moral perfection" by identifying twelve virtues that he wanted to master. He strived towards temperance, silence, order, resolution, frugality, industry, sincerity, justice, moderation, cleanliness, tranquility, and chastity.

As he worked on his list of virtues, Franklin asked a friend for some input. The friend suggested Franklin was missing one more key virtue: humility. He explained that Franklin came across as "generally thought proud" and "overbearing and rather insolent," providing specific examples of when this pride had shown up. Displaying unusual open-mindedness, Franklin made humility his thirteenth virtue. He then put together a detailed schedule to work on the thirteen virtues one at time over thirteen weeks, repeating the cycle four times per year. He tracked his progress by creating a log book and making a black mark each time he perceived himself to have failed to exhibit a given virtue. Franklin devised a well-thought-out plan to change his actions and words to try to get closer to these virtues; his discipline in reflecting on his own thinking and values and the perseverance in improving himself are valuable lessons that today's leaders would do well to learn.

"I Need to Spend More Time Alone"

We have seen so far that to gain more humility, a leader needs to reflect on their own personality traits, emotional intelligence, world views, and values. Unfortunately, the hustle and bustle of busy executive life is a major obstacle to this type of reflection, which requires, more than anything, alone time. A study examining the daily calendars of CEOs found that they spend only 28 percent of their time at work alone, with the rest spent in meetings. And what do most CEOs do when they are by themselves? You guessed it: email.

Take the example of Tom Gentile, one of the CEOs included in the study. Gentile became the CEO of Spirit AeroSystems—a large aerostructures manufacturer—in August 2016. A few months into his tenure, over a period of thirteen weeks, his executive assistant tracked his days in fifteen-minute increments, including where he was, whom he was with, and what he was focusing on. Gentile's average workweek, including commute and travel, amounted to a whopping 73.5 hours. Not unlike other CEOs, he spent very little of that time alone. Even when he wasn't in the company of others, he didn't pause to think and reflect. Instead, he spent the majority of his alone time tending to email messages.

When the researchers dug a bit deeper into the data, they discovered that Gentile wasn't intentional in protecting any large blocks of alone time. The majority of the time he spent by himself was in thirty-minute increments or less, which made him more likely to use that time for electronic communication than for deep thinking. "I . . . need to spend more time alone, thinking and being proactive. My blocks of unscheduled time are too short for me to be reflective about big issues, and I tend to just go to my in-box," he remarked. The only time that he spent alone with no distractions was while he was driving or when he found himself on an airplane with no WiFi signal. If you are like Gentile, you need to be deliberate in blocking large chunks of uninterrupted time alone in order to have time for reflection about yourself and the issues you are dealing with. In other words, you need to engineer solitude or "heads-up" time into your days.

Solitude is not a state that leaders commonly seek or value. When I talk about solitude with executives in my workshops, the concept makes most of them uncomfortable. They remark that they can't stand being by themselves or that they don't like the feeling of being alone, even for a few minutes. So when they do find themselves alone, they don't want to think about deep issues—they just want to watch some mindless TV show or TikTok videos. "A crowded world thinks that aloneness is loneliness and that to seek it is perversion," remarked the author John Graves, and the research supports that view.

In a well-known study, participants were placed in empty rooms and their cellphones and other belongings were taken away from them. For intervals of up to fifteen minutes, some were asked to think about whatever they wanted, and others to react to specific prompts, such as going out to eat or playing a sport. When asked to rate their experience, more than half of the participants in both groups reported low levels of enjoyment and high levels of boredom. In the second part, the researchers took the experiment to the next level. They left each participant alone for fifteen minutes in a laboratory room to think with no prompts, and also gave them the option to push a button that would discharge an electric shock if they felt inclined to do so. Inexplicably, about 67 percent of the male participants and 25 percent of the female participants pushed the button! They actually preferred the experience of being shocked with electricity over that of sitting quietly and thinking. In the previously mentioned CEO calendar study, the equivalent of the electric shock is reading and answering emails—even the dreadful task of dealing with a full inbox is more attractive for leaders than reflection.

When you think of a leader, you might imagine them surrounded by other people in a large conference room, strategizing and giving orders. But the importance of alone time cannot be overemphasized if you are serious about understanding yourself and your world. "It is difficult to understand yourself if you are never by yourself," noted Ryan Holiday in his book *Stillness Is the Key*. In that same book, four-star Marine Corps general and former secretary of defense Jim Mattis noted that the single biggest problem of senior leadership today is lack of reflection. When you are constantly in the company of others, it is almost impossible for you to think clearly. And when thinking time is rare, you hardly have any opportunity to understand the issues, let alone understand your own beliefs, values, strengths, or weaknesses.

While humans are undoubtedly social beings, they also have a need to be by themselves. According to psychologists, connecting with others and being alone are both essential. Seeking solitude is not the same as being antisocial. When you block time on your calendars to be by yourself, you are not just meeting a basic human need, you are also allowing yourself to show up better when you reconnect with your stakeholders. Alone time also allows you to have fresher ideas and to be more creative. When the scholar Anthony Storr analyzed the lives of great artists and writers, such as Beethoven, Dostoyevsky, and Kafka, he found that most of their innovative ideas came after they retreated from others and intentionally spent time by themselves. In addition to creativity, knowledge and understanding of the self are major benefits of solitude. Storr believed that solitude "promotes self-understanding and contact with those inner depths of being" to a degree impossible to achieve in day-to-day life.

Heads-Up vs. Heads-Down

How should you go about building solitude into your schedule? And what exactly should you be doing when you are alone? First, you should use your solitude time productively, with a particular end in mind. This type of productive solitude requires you to work your mind actively by breaking down and synthesizing your thoughts and feelings. To achieve this, you need to purposefully isolate yourself from the external world. Limit the inputs that you are receiving from the outside in the form of emails, text messages, or notifications. An hour spent reading the news or scrolling through Facebook is not exactly deep reflection time. With so much information coming at you, you need to figure out how to "filter out the inconsequential from the essential," according to Holiday. Nate Fick, a former Marine Recon officer and the CEO of a firm specializing in cyber-threat defenses, intentionally reduces his inputs and creates time and space for sober thought and analysis. For example, he recently replaced the phone in his office with a 1970s rotary phone so he does not get distracted by the blinking light of new voice messages. He also tells his assistant that he needs ninety minutes a day on his calendar to close the door and think. Additionally, he sets the tone for others in his organization by requiring them to take two days each month to think and reflect, with no meetings allowed.

If you are an extrovert who derives your energy from being with other people, you are probably not convinced that solitude is for you. A better concept for you may be "heads-up" time, which is a term I learned at MEDI, a large healthcare-specific coaching company. The analogy that my fellow coaches at MEDI use is that of walking on a mountain trail. As you make your way from point A to point B, you need to watch where you are stepping or you could trip on a rock or fall off a cliff—so you keep your eyes on the path. This is referred to as "heads-down" time, and it is the state in which people spend most of their days at work: they pay attention to making the right moves, avoiding mistakes, and handling mini-crises. However, if you never stop and raise your head while you are walking, you won't know where you are going and you will certainly miss the beauty of the mountain view and the majesty of the experience. The same applies to work: heads-up time is the time you take to think deeply and reflect—whether by yourself or with the help of a small team.

The most productive time spent in thinking and reflection for a leader, then, is time that includes no electronics or screens, and preferably time when they are equipped with a pen and a blank page of paper. A very productive habit of high-performing leaders who are deliberate in getting to know themselves is journaling. I was once visiting with Deneese Jones, the academic vice president we met earlier, in her office. In addition to the numerous books neatly lined up on the shelves, I also noticed a section in the corner of the office with what looked like hundreds of leather notebooks. I asked her about them and she explained that these were her leadership journals. "I've been reflecting on my leadership ever since I became a leader thirty years ago," she said. I asked her whether she goes back to look at some of the older journals. "All the time!" she exclaimed. "I get a lot of value from looking at how I used to think and approach situations twenty years ago, ten years ago, and how I do it now. These journals are a gold mine!" Journaling allows us to better understand ourselves and the issues that we face every day. The author Julia Cameron insightfully compared journaling to windshield wipers that swipe away at the things that stand between us and a clear view of our days and lives.

Let me stress that journaling in specific and self-reflection in general need to be done the right way, or they could lead to *reduced* self-awareness. A major determinant of whether self-reflection is productive or not is the type of questions that you ask yourself when you are reflecting: questions that start with "why" typically lead to unproductive rumination, whereas those that start with "what" are more likely to lead to objective analyses that focus on the future and empower you to act.

In one study at the University of Texas at Austin, undergraduate students were given negative feedback about their personalities. Half the students were assigned to the *why* condition that required them to think about the question, "Why are you the kind of person you are in terms of sociability, likability, and interestingness?" The other half were assigned to the *what* condition and were asked to think about the question, "What kind of person are you in terms of sociability, likability, and interestingness?" The results showed that the opportunity to introspect promoted self-insight among those in the *what* condition, but not in the *why* condition. The researchers concluded that "thinking about why one is the way one is may be no better than not thinking about one's self at all." Some executive coaches I discussed this study with agreed with the findings and also noted that *why* questions tend to invoke defensiveness among their coachees. Especially when things aren't going well, *what* questions such as, "What could I have done differently to achieve a different outcome?" are much more fruitful.

So productive self-reflection is about asking yourself questions that will allow you to grow as a leader and move forward by taking action. For example, in your journal, consider reflecting on questions such as:

- What do I need to do to avoid standing in my own way?

- What's the smallest step I can take towards a big thing today?

- What am I so worked up about?

- What blessings can I count right now?

· What should I do to care less about impressing other people?

Keep a notebook with you at all times, and when the opportunity for reflection arises in between meetings or on a long flight, try wrestling with these types of questions. Some of the great leaders throughout history have kept journals that allowed them to reflect on a regular basis. For example, in the midst of World War II, General Dwight Eisenhower regularly wrote notes to himself. Eisenhower's journaling allowed him to gain better self-insight, which resulted in clarity about the key decisions that he was about to make.

Make the Time

One alternative to sitting down and writing is going for a walk. Tom Gentile, the busy CEO we met before, admitted that while detaching from his email was hard for him, he did start walking around his company headquarters more often. Obviously, it is hard for leaders to find the time and setting for a walk, and that's why walks need to be planned and built even into an already-packed schedule. The advantage walking provides is that while the body is engaged in repetitive, controlled movement, the mind can wander around on its own and thoughts can emerge with no effort. Nietzsche was surely exaggerating when he claimed that "it is only ideas gained from walking that have any worth," but he had a point. Sometimes, though, going for a walk is not physically possible, especially if you are leading in a war zone. Retired four-star Army general Stanley McChrystal, whom we will hear more from later in this book, related that during the Iraq War, he often found solitude in the air: "Helicopter rides were good for thinking about decisions. I'd put the headphones on. No one can mess with you. Not getting emails. Just watching the brown terrain passing by below, hour after hour, I felt centered."

Another habit you can adopt is dedicating time for reading and reflecting on what you read. As Tolstoy noted a long time ago, when we read, we give ourselves the opportunity to communicate with the wisest people who ever lived on earth. Some successful leaders I interact with tell me they block thirty to forty-five minutes, typically every morning or evening, to read business and leadership books, as well as other types of books and articles that prod them to think deeper. Glenn Robinson, the successful CEO of a large hospital in Hillcrest, Texas, and a common guest speaker in our graduate program at Trinity University, always advises young leaders that if they want to be in the top 5 percent of their field, they have to dedicate time for reading every day. Many young and seasoned leaders admit, though, that while they would like to read more, they don't have time for it. When you say that you don't have time to read, what you are really saying is that you haven't made reading a priority in your day and haven't blocked time to allow yourself to do it. In his practical and entertaining book *Your Oxygen Mask First*, executive coach Kevin Lawrence says, "When leaders tell me they're way too busy to invest time in learning, I tell them being stupid is expensive and dangerous. Make the time."

How can busy leaders find the time to read? In a popular *Harvard Business Review* article, Canadian author Neil Pasricha recommends several different ways to read more each year. His practical suggestions include making a public commitment on social media, finding a few trusted curated lists of books by people you admire, quitting books you don't like without feeling guilty about it, and canceling newspaper and magazine subscriptions and spending that time and money on books. Moreover, Pasricha shares that he took his TV down to his dark, unfinished basement and replaced it with a bookshelf. Pasricha also hosts a podcast called *Three Books*, for which he is on a thirteen-year quest to uncover the thousand most formative books ever. Recent research supports the call for leaders to invest more time in reading. A study of 6,500 executives revealed that the top-performing leaders read an average of twenty-four books per year, equally divided between fiction and non-fiction.

But reading by itself is not enough: it has to be complemented by taking notes, reflecting, and setting actionable goals. As an author and researcher, I naturally read many books. I have noticed, though, that when I read a book without highlighting the important parts and transcribing them later to a separate document, I often remember very little from the book. That is why I now keep neon highlighters with me everywhere, and I later transcribe the notes. I agree with Kevin Lawrence: "If you finish a book ... without a list of to-dos, with all due respect, what was the point? You might as well have gone to a movie."

One practice that I hear a lot about from leaders, especially those with long commutes or extensive travel schedules, is listening to audiobooks. Some have told me they buy both the audiobook and hard copy. After they listen to the audiobook, if something really catches their attention or connects with them, they go back to that chapter in the hard copy and underline the sentences or record the insights in their journals.

While all of the practices we've discussed so far include allocating blocks of time here and there, sometimes you just need to be bold and dedicate a few days in a row for an annual personal retreat. You are familiar with company strategic planning retreats or team off-sites, but perhaps you have never considered doing the same activity by yourself. The most famous personal retreat is probably Bill Gates's semi-annual "Think Week," a stretch of solitude in a cabin in the middle of a cedar forest somewhere in the Pacific Northwest. During these seven days in solitude, Gates reads articles and books for up to eighteen hours per day. He analyzes what he reads, and writes copious notes. Based on his analyses, he makes decisions about future projects that Microsoft should pursue. While Gates's focus is mostly on his company, you can adopt a similar approach by dedicating a certain number of days per year to focus inwards and reflect on your achievements, mistakes, and areas for improvement. An annual personal retreat is definitely time well spent, and if Gates can find the time to do it, you have no excuse. Once you build a habit of reflection, you will notice your performance improving and that your decisions are better-informed.

The Stories We Tell Ourselves

So far, we have discussed the importance of self-reflection and deep-thinking time for leaders, but we haven't made a clear connection yet with humility. Solitude enables you to obtain the clarity and fierce resolve that allow the seeds of humbitious leadership to start developing. In a recent email exchange, Ryan Holiday explained to me how stillness, a calm state that inspires reflection and sharpens perspective, is directly related to humility: "When you practice stillness, you cultivate confidence in yourself and a connectedness to other people, as opposed to just focusing on your ego."

Self-reflection practices and questions can help you improve your humility, especially after a remarkable success. When you force yourself to reflect on where you came from, that humility enables you to remain grounded after a big promotion or major accomplishment. Harry Kraemer, a successful CEO and professor, intentionally and periodically reminds himself of his beginnings: "Like many people I started my career in a cubicle. It was small, not much more than six feet by six feet, and if I moved my chair back too quickly, I hit my head on the metal filing cabinet directly behind me... No matter what positions of responsibility I later had the privilege of holding, I won't forget where I came from: the six-by-six workspace I affectionately call 'the cube.'" Reflecting on where you started your career, whether that was in a small cubicle or a fast-food joint, allows you to gain a valuable perspective.

When you self-reflect after successes, you gain humility by acknowledging that, in addition to your strengths, skills, and hard work, other key factors, such as luck and timing, played a significant role in your success. While humility pushes you to be more honest with yourself, pride and arrogance push you to make up stories and lie to yourself. It is important to remember that pride is considered a sin in most religions because, at its core, to be prideful is to lie. You lie to yourself and others about how good you are. If you are a non-reflective, prideful leader, you may tell yourself stories about your own success: "I planned it like this from the beginning," "I knew it all along," or "I succeeded because I'm just that good." However, honest self-reflection will likely cause you to change your self-story and admit to yourself: "I hoped it would work but I wasn't sure," "I worked hard but I also got some lucky breaks," and "I got a lot of help from my team." In these moments of true self-reflection, some important questions to ask yourself include:

- Who trained and mentored me?

- Who schedules my meetings and manages my calendar?

- How many people on my team and in my organization are doing a great job?

- How did luck and market conditions contribute to my success?

As a humbitious leader, while you recognize the role of other factors in your successes, make sure that you do not minimize the importance of these successes. Chloe Banker and Mark Leary from Duke University recently designed a study to examine how humble people view their own successes. They asked participants to describe all kinds of personal characteristics or accomplishments they were proud of. The results showed that people who are more humble in nature do in fact acknowledge the importance of their own positive characteristics and accomplishments and think of them as special. However, they do not believe that they are entitled to be treated differently by others because of those special characteristics and accomplishments. As we have noted so far, humble people, due to their habit of honest self-reflection, see themselves more accurately than other people and as a result know what they are and are not good at. The core feature of humility, then, is not downplaying your strengths, but rather not believing that you should be treated differently because of them—a trait the researchers called "hypo-egoic non-entitlement." (Yes, academics do love to make up a lot of big words.)

One final thought: self-reflection, sober analysis, and honestly questioning your assumptions and stories is hard work. And that is why it should be habitual work that you do every day. It is like sweeping the floor in a dusty room: just because you did it yesterday, that doesn't mean that the floor will remain clean forever. You have to do it today, and come back to do it again tomorrow, and every day.

What Next?

To sum it up: being humble means being aware of your shortcomings as well as your strengths, and you can't be aware without taking time to look at yourself and reflect on your life and actions—and to learn from others. Here is a short list of action items for this:

- Work with a coach to better understand your personality traits and emotional intelligence strengths and weaknesses.

- Deliberately reflect on your values, beliefs, and world views.

- Seek solitude by blocking off reasonable blocks of alone time. Schedule time, then commit to keeping it.

- Consider journaling periodically and asking yourself "what" types of questions.

- Start small. If thirty minutes of reflection seems like too much, start with five minutes and increase it as you go.

- Plan daily or weekly walks for thinking and reflection.

- Adopt a regular reading habit. As you are reading, highlight important passages, write them down, and reflect on them later on.

· Reflect on your successes and the role that luck, external forces, and your team members have played in allowing you to achieve those successes.

With a better understanding of your shortcomings, you are now well positioned to share your limitations with others. In the next chapter, we will investigate the importance of being comfortable with vulnerability.

— 6 —

Vulnerability

*Humility offers self-understanding. When we
acknowledge that we screw up, and feel the gravity of
our limitations, we find ourselves challenged and
stretched with a serious foe to overcome and transcend.*

DAVID BROOKS

ENUF

"Today, even though it's Friday, I'm not feeling it . . . Why? I think it's ENUF! (exhausting, never-ending, useless, frustrations) . . . We aren't our usual selves. That's ok—frankly it's more than ok. It's normal to be a little 'off' these days from time to time . . . We have to look at it—understand it —forgive ourselves for not being perfect and find the joy & the fun & the truth that life right now is hard as heck. Leadership in easy times is not for the faint of heart, and now is definitely not easy. So keep moving forward, doing your best. It's enough!"

If you had read this on a friend's Facebook page, you might not have thought much about it. Your friend is sharing some personal stuff, but there is nothing unusual about the post itself. But this post is not by one of your friends, and it is not on Facebook. It is what Janice Kaffer, president and CEO of

Hôtel-Dieu Grace Healthcare, a community hospital with a network of clinics and community-based services in Ontario (and a leader we met earlier in this book), recently posted on her professional LinkedIn page. This is not the first time she has made a post like this. Janice regularly shares how she is feeling and bravely discusses sensitive issues such as gender discrimination, mental health, and politics.

The common thread among all of Janice's social media posts is that she is not afraid to be vulnerable. Her team members and employees love her authenticity and transparency, which extends beyond her social media feeds and into her personal interactions. Judy Wyllie, one of her team members, explains: "Jan has a great connection to our people, because she embraces vulnerability by sharing herself with us, in her very own 'Jan' way, fearlessly and compassionately. We know her as our CEO and as a wife, mother, and grandmother, what keeps her up at night and the very many ways she is so proud of our people."

A couple of years ago, Janice's organization invited me to give a talk, and that is when I got to know her personally. Later on, I asked her about the source of her humble and vulnerable leadership brand. She reflected that, having raised her kids on a farm, she has always worked hard and appreciated that life is difficult. She came to her CEO position with that appreciation. She knows how challenging life is for her employees because she was a nurse herself early in her career. She realizes that people are not just workers, they are human beings with lives. "This is the place from which I lead. I do not try to separate work from life," she explained. She brings her grandchildren with her to work and she is very open about her limitations. When she is having personal conversations with employees, she doesn't shy away from sharing the struggles that some of her family members have had with addiction. She talks about post-partum depression, loss, and grief. "I don't want to be a talking head," she told me. "When people are connected to their leader and to their work, they are more engaged and they give more discretionary effort."

In another recent post, Janice demonstrated her humbition when she openly reflected on things she wished she had known when she first became CEO. She described how, when she started in her position, she had thought that a CEO had to be perfect. When she made her first mistake, she was devastated and became consumed with self-doubt. But then she started to learn to be okay with making mistakes. "Learn from it, fix it & grow to be a better leader from it," she wrote. Janice believes that she only recently found her voice on social media. Her social media voice and CEO voice are one and the same because she believes it is too exhausting to pretend to be what you are not. She is intentional about being authentic, and her sense of humor shows up from time to time. She does not want to sound "too corporate" on social media, but she also guards against "being too 'me.'" She has a rule to not tweet after the second glass of wine.

Janice Kaffer provides us with a powerful example of how humbitious leaders can show vulnerability and authenticity while still being accountable and holding others to high standards. Under her leadership, her organization has achieved excellent outcomes as one of the leading healthcare organizations in Canada. Let us explore in depth how vulnerability, the last step in understanding yourself, can be helpful for you as a humbitious leader.

The Charade of Perfection

In the last two chapters, we discussed the importance of self-awareness and self-reflection for leaders. While it is crucial for you to understand your strengths and weaknesses, as a humbitious leader, you also have to take it a step further by appropriately sharing your weaknesses, as well as your shortcomings and mistakes, with others. You need to recognize that you are human first and foremost, and, like all human beings, you are not perfect. You have anxieties and challenges, you don't know everything, and you need help.

This is why you should not shy away from demonstrating fallibility, vulnerability, and transparency. Make sure you show up every day in an authentic way: avoid seeking perfection, apologize and take ownership when you err or miscalculate, and ask for others' support. Just like Janice Kaffer, work on bringing your whole self to your work, and share your struggles and difficulties without worrying about appearing weak or inadequate. Let's uncover what it means to be fallible, vulnerable, and transparent, and how these behaviors relate to humbitious leadership. We will discuss the benefits of leading in this courageous way, but also explain the necessary boundaries you need to put in place to avoid oversharing and losing credibility.

Let us first start with the opposite of vulnerability, namely, the pursuit of perfection. Leaders who have an inflated ego wrongly believe they need to appear perfect, powerful, decisive, and fearless—*all the time*. Harvard professor Chris Argyris argued that these beliefs are related to underlying values that many unaware people have. They wrongly assume they need to be constantly in control, to maximize winning, to avoid all negative feelings, and to be rational. He explains that "the purpose of all these values is to avoid embarrassment or threat, feeling vulnerable or incompetent." Such values manifest themselves in ineffective leadership behaviors, such as feigning confidence when unsure, hiding confusion about puzzling results, and suppressing feelings of inadequacy when coping with complex issues. "Never let them see you sweat" is a saying these leaders often live by. They have convinced themselves of "the myth of the complete leader," the flawless person who has it all figured out.

The reason why these beliefs, values, and behaviors are counterproductive is that they can lead to self-destruction. Ironically, if you buy into the lie of being perfect, you subconsciously set yourself up for career derailment. You cover up mistakes and do not own up to failures. You blame others for problems and avoid taking responsibility. You do not spend the time to reflect on experiences and you miss the opportunity to learn and improve. You hopelessly try to hold a façade, while everyone around you knows that you are struggling and pretending. As a result, you eventually fall. In contrast, if you start with humbitiousness, you give yourself the permission to be fallible, vulnerable, and transparent, and, as a result, you set yourself up for success.

In their remarkable book chapter on humility, Erik Hoekstra, current president of Dordt University, and his colleagues argue that fallibility, vulnerability, and transparency are among the foundations of humble leadership. To start with, they note that "embracing an appropriate fallibility, the leader is freed from living out the charade of perfectionism and the façade of never being wrong." Fallibility starts with you as a leader admitting to your followers: "I make mistakes." This is not simply about saying that mistakes happen and they're just part of life. It is about recognizing that followers do not expect any leader to be perfect. As a result, you need to ask your team members for their patience. This creates an authenticity that is appealing and attractive to others. Since everyone knows that leaders make mistakes, your followers are already aware that you are not an exception.

While fallibility is hard, vulnerability is even harder. Vulnerability is not just about admitting that you make mistakes in general, it is about admitting specific mistakes and asking for forgiveness. As a vulnerable leader, you say to your followers, "I was wrong." You ask for forgiveness from those who were affected by your actions, and you reflect on how you contributed to the problem or crisis. It is not enough to say, "Yeah, that was a mistake," or "Something went wrong." You should offer a specific acknowledgment and a focused apology. The interesting thing about vulnerability is that it leads to significant trust, and the relationship between you and your team members can go forward without any residual pain or ill will. When you declare your humanness and admit to making mistakes, it is refreshing and even endearing for the people around you.

Deneese Jones, the leader we met in previous chapters, explained to me that, early on in her career, she felt the need to hide mistakes and build walls in order to protect herself. However, as her confidence, humility, and desire to help others grew, she realized the importance of fallibility and vulnerability. When I met with her at her house in the fall of 2019, she shared a story about a recent mistake she had made when preparing the university budget. "I came clean and I told the department chair who was affected that I was sorry, I made a mistake. Before, she was very angry with me. But after I apologized, she suddenly softened. She said: 'I never worked with someone who had admitted their mistakes before!' Now when she sees me, she goes out of her way, she hugs me and she talks to me, and she wants us to have lunch!"

If there is one person responsible for popularizing the idea of vulnerability and making it part of the leadership lexicon, it is Brené Brown, from the University of Houston. In her best-selling book *Dare to Lead*, Brown defined vulnerability in similar ways to what we have discussed so far in this chapter: apologizing, admitting mistakes, taking risks, and facing uncertainty. A vulnerable leader is one who gives up on the idea of perfectionism and instead focuses on being their authentic self. Let me make it clear, though: abandoning the pursuit of perfection is not synonymous with giving up on self-improvement and striving to be your best. In a less well-known book, aptly titled *The Gifts of Imperfection*, Brown explains that healthy striving is self-focused and often asks the question, "How can I improve?" Perfectionism, on the other hand, is other-focused and is mainly concerned with, "What will they think?" Similarly, perfectionism is about hiding your weaknesses so you can avoid the pain of shame, while striving to be your best is about healthy achievement and growth.

Black Jeans and Turtlenecks

Compare and contrast authenticity with the example of Elizabeth Holmes, the founder of Theranos, a company that promised to revolutionize healthcare. Holmes dropped out of Stanford at age nineteen to work on a blood-testing technology that she imagined could diagnose chronic diseases such as diabetes and cancer with just one drop of blood. In a famous TED Talk, she announced, "If I had one wish, standing here with all of you, it would be that today, just for a minute, you think about the fact that we have this right, a human right, to engage with information about ourselves, about our bodies, and for those that we love to engage with information about themselves. And when we do that, we will change our lives, and the lives of those we love will change."

She often claimed that her uncle's death from cancer was the reason she founded her company—she wanted to create a "world in which no one ever has to say goodbye too soon." She presented herself as the benevolent founder who just wanted to help others.

As it turns out, it was all lies and deceit. Holmes was just chasing money and fame, and Theranos never really had a working product. She lied to board members and investors, raising $400 million in total while leading doctors and patients to believe that her technology actually worked. She even convinced Walgreens to put the devices in its stores by falsely claiming that they had been comprehensively tested by large pharmaceutical companies. When Theranos started testing patient blood at the Walgreens locations in Arizona, the unreliable results put numerous patients' lives at risk. But Holmes didn't care.

One of the major flaws in Elizabeth Holmes's leadership was her lack of authenticity. She worshipped Steve Jobs and believed herself to be his heir in Silicon Valley. She called her product the iPod of healthcare and predicted that it would be in every household, just like Apple products are. Someone once told her that if she wanted to be like Steve Jobs, she had to look the part. So she replaced her baggy clothes with black jeans and turtlenecks, to mimic how the Apple founder dressed. She also spoke with a fake deep voice, though occasionally, when she got really excited, she inadvertently reverted to her normal voice—to the surprise of the people who were around her.

Holmes was finally exposed by a *Wall Street Journal* investigation and is awaiting trial. At the time of writing, Theranos, the company that promised to change the world, does not exist anymore. If convicted, Holmes could face up to twenty years in prison.

"We're in the Paper!"

Unlike Holmes, humbitious leaders understand the importance of an authentic apology when needed. In March of 2018, Doug Lawson was still working on figuring out how to make his new parking pass work when one of his team members ominously told him: "We're in the paper!" For any leader, these are scary words. And for a leader just starting at the highest position in a new organization, there is nothing more frightening. Lawson, a humbitious leader known for his intelligence, experience, and strategic thinking, had just accepted the position of CEO at Catholic Health Initiatives' Texas Division, a large network of twenty hospitals serving Houston, East Texas, and the Brazos Valley. He couldn't help but wonder what mess he was stepping into.

A few months before Lawson came on board, several patients undergoing heart transplants at Baylor St. Luke's Medical Center, the division's flagship hospital, had suffered complications and deaths that were deemed to be preventable. The *Houston Chronicle* launched an investigation of those incidents and published a series of long articles documenting the errors under the title "Heart Failure." For the general public, this came as a huge surprise. St. Luke's had a stellar reputation built on the legacies of the famous surgeon Denton Cooley, who had performed one of the world's first heart transplants in the 1960s, and of physician O.H. "Bud" Frazier, who developed a mechanical replacement for the human heart. Decades later, the hospital continued to flaunt these achievements, despite the fact that the survival rates for St. Luke's heart transplants were ranked near the bottom nationally, according to publicly reported data. Patients were staying in the hospital for weeks or months after their transplants, which indicated possible complications occurring at a much higher rate than in other transplant programs.

"I didn't realize how bad things were until CMS [the Center for Medicare and Medicaid] did a review in January of 2019 which was very concerning," explained Lawson as we had lunch in his office a few months later. After the report came out, Lawson knew that the hospital needed to regain the trust of the public and of its own physicians and employees. "It was clear that I needed to create a burning platform for change across the organization. I felt very strongly that it was time for the organization to take ownership of these issues and demonstrate our commitment to making real and substantive changes. By making the whole report available, we were sending a very clear signal that the status quo was no longer acceptable," he explained. On February 26, 2019, in a highly unusual move for a healthcare CEO, Lawson wrote an apology letter that he published on his own social media feeds, as well as on St. Luke's platforms and website.

"When I recently stepped into the role of Baylor St. Luke's Medical Center President, I made a series of commitments to our patients and their families, to our staff and physicians, and to the broader Houston community," the letter started. "Today, however, I'm sharing results... of a patient death following a blood transfusion error in the Emergency Department... It is our responsibility to learn from these mistakes, and we take this responsibility very seriously. An incident like this should never happen."

In his letter, Lawson shared the full CMS report, as well as the hospital's plan to correct the deficiencies, including wholesale changes in clinical and administrative leadership positions. He ended by offering hope, promising that the organization would regain its patients' trust and take the steps needed to ensure it fulfilled its mission of care and compassion. Within a few hours of publication, the letter went viral, with thousands of views and hundreds of comments all over social media. And Lawson started the journey of leading the organization back to its famed past of excellent patient care.

It is clear that Doug Lawson took ownership of a problem that had occurred long before he joined the organization. However, he did not blame his predecessors or point the fingers at others in order to make himself look good. In their remarkable book *Extreme Ownership*, U.S. Navy SEAL officers Jocko Willink and Leif Babin explain that, even if it is not your fault, as a leader you have to take responsibility. Anything that happens for you, for your team, and for your organization is your responsibility. There are no excuses for mistakes or poor performance. You can't blame the old team, bad luck, the volatile economy, resource-rich competitors, or incompetent employees. Willink and Babin propose the same position as Lawson took: "The leader must own everything in his or her world. There is no one else to blame."

How can you resist the temptation to come up with excuses and avoid responsibility? You have to be humble. Even in the best-trained combat unit in the world, high-performing leaders display humility. They put the mission above their personal needs, and accept the suggestions and ideas of their team members. "Ego clouds and disrupts everything," Willink and Babin explain. It impacts your ability to plan, to take good advice, and to accept constructive criticism. The connection between humility and taking ownership for mistakes is strongly supported by the evidence. Humble people are less inclined to take advantage of others and are not especially concerned about their perceived status being negatively affected by the apology. Moreover, since taking ownership and apologizing are humbling experiences, they tend to come more naturally to people who are more humble in nature.

"I Don't Know"

I was recently listening to an interview with the acclaimed author Ta-Nehisi Coates as part of the Civil Conversations project. An audience member asked him for advice on how history should be taught in schools. "I don't know," came the honest reply. Coates explained that he was never a good student, and so he had no advice on how to teach. The audience laughed and was still expecting him to answer the question. But then he added, "I'm serious, because one of the things that annoys me is, people act like they know everything ... Come on, be clear about what you know and what you don't know." I strongly believe that, as a leader, you ought to follow this advice and transparently admit to what you know and don't know.

In addition to fallibility and vulnerability, a major foundation of humble leadership is transparency. While fallibility and vulnerability are about admitting mistakes and taking ownership, transparency focuses on admitting that you have weaknesses and shortcomings, and that sometimes, you just don't know the answer. I share Coates's annoyance with the know-it-alls, especially in organizations. These are the people who lack humility and are always ready to offer an opinion or to explain things to everyone around them. When put in positions of power, these types of people then require all information to flow through them. They make it obligatory for themselves to sign off on all big and small decisions, and as a result, they become bottlenecks for ideas.

Humbitious leaders, on the other hand, have no problem with sometimes admitting they don't know, as well as with decentralizing decision-making in their teams and organizations. They tell their team members, "I need your ideas." When followers see a leader admitting their shortcomings and knowledge gaps, they respond by bringing their best thinking, thus unleashing collaboration, innovation, and creative thinking, which are all documented benefits of humbitious leadership, as we saw in Chapter 2.

Brad Smith, the former CEO of Intuit, a financial software company, asked his board for a 360-degree assessment as soon as he started in his position. But he didn't stop there; he actually shared the results of the assessment, especially the weaknesses, with the entire company. He even taped up a copy of the report to make sure everyone saw it. "Each year I created clear development goals that I shared with other rising stars in the leadership pipeline. This created a safe space for them to become more reflective and self-aware. People started checking their egos at the door and asking for help," he clarified. As I read about Smith's transparency in a recent *Harvard Business Review* article, I couldn't help but compare him with some of the egocentric leaders I've interacted with over the years. For some of these, just the idea of a 360-degree assessment sends shivers down their spines. The way they see it, the 360 means that, God forbid, people are going to talk about their imperfections and weaknesses!

In addition to unleashing collaboration and creating safety and trust, another major benefit of sharing insecurities is that it prevents you from sweeping these issues under the rug and running the risk of having them show their ugly heads at the wrong time. When you hide your anxieties, they may arise during a big presentation or just before you make a decision, which will invariably have a negative impact on your performance. Eileen Murray, a former executive at the large hedge fund Bridgewater, made it a point to encourage young leaders in her organization to become more comfortable talking about their fears and limitations. She regularly scheduled 1:1 coaching sessions with talented individuals whom she considered rising stars, and she would start these meetings by sharing her own anxieties and fears. For example, she might describe to them how she was feeling when she became the first woman to lead the organization: "You can imagine all of the fears swirling around in my head: fear of looking stupid, fear of getting fired for making a bad decision, fear of saying something that got perversely twisted in the press, fear of letting down my board of directors. I openly shared my angst with subordinates. I was an open book. Honesty is the cornerstone for all trusting relationships, and it had to start with me." By helping young leaders feel safe to talk about their concerns, Murray was building a culture of transparency, growth, and humbition.

Ordinary Courage

We have shown so far that fallibility, vulnerability, and transparency are key to leadership success. How do you go about developing these traits? The evidence seems to point towards a combination of humility and courage. It starts with your ego.

An inflated ego is dependent on how others view you and is wrapped up in being right all the time, which prevents vulnerability. Humility, on the other hand, allows your ego to free itself from depending on others' recognition and to focus more on growth. It allows you to be vulnerable to the possibility of not knowing it all and to having someone else teach you something new. You become more open to experimentation and open the door for the people around you to give you feedback and propose new ideas. My colleague and executive coach Lee Angus told me about a new CEO he once coached whose ego was so big that it prevented him from showing any signs of vulnerability. The CEO built a wall around himself and wanted to show that he was right all the time. None of his team members dared give him any feedback or offer any suggestions. Not surprisingly, he didn't last longer than six months in his position.

As we have seen so far, humility that leads to vulnerability is not a sign of weakness. In fact, "it requires a 'unique sort of courage' to be willing to be vulnerable for the sake of personal development and growth for the self and others," as Brad Owens notes. What kind of courage are we talking about? It is not about big acts of heroism, but rather about everyday courage, where you speak openly and honestly about who you are. Brené Brown explains that "ordinary courage is about putting our vulnerability on the line." For example, saying "I don't know" in a meeting when you suspect that everyone around you knows the answer requires a lot of courage. But it is only when you cultivate that courage to be imperfect and when you allow yourself to be vulnerable that you can show up in a truly authentic way to every conversation and meeting.

It is also important to note, as Brown reminds us, that while there is no vulnerability without courage, there is no courage without discomfort. As a humbitious leader, you need to recognize that you cannot move yourself, your team, and your organization in the right direction while staying comfortable. To grow, and to challenge yourself and your followers, you have to learn to become comfortable with discomfort. In order to model this behavior to others, practice saying, "Wow, this is making me a bit uncomfortable, but it is very important for us to discuss it," or, "I know this conversation is making some people uncomfortable, but I would like you all to express your opinions because it's worth it."

Courage is also a major prerequisite for apologizing and owning up to mistakes. One interesting psychological phenomenon that takes place in your brain when you make a mistake is called *cognitive dissonance*. When you do something wrong or cross a moral line, you tend to justify the behavior that you know is wrong so you can continue to see yourself as a good person. Over time, you start believing your own little lies. But self-justification is not the same thing as lying or making excuses. When you lie or make excuses, you know you are lying to others to save your skin. In self-justification, you lie to yourself. That is why self-justification is far more dangerous: it tricks you. "There was nothing else I could have done," we tell ourselves.

Cognitive dissonance is the energy that drives this self-justification. It is the state of tension that occurs whenever you hold two cognitions (ideas, attitudes, beliefs, or opinions) that are psychologically inconsistent. Dissonance produces mental discomfort that will not go away until you find a way to reduce it. For example, a manager may think of himself as a reasonable, calm person. However, when he confronts a direct report about a mistake during a meeting, he loses his cool and yells in front of everyone. The two ideas of *I am*

normally reasonable and calm and *I yelled in front of everyone*
create cognitive dissonance. So instead of admitting the
mistake and apologizing to the team and employee, the boss
reduces his mental discomfort by convincing himself that
there was nothing else he could have done. "I had to yell at
him, otherwise he would never learn," he repeats to himself.

In their remarkable book *Mistakes Were Made (but Not by
Me)*, social psychologists Carol Tavris and Elliot Aronson note
that one of the ways to overcome cognitive dissonance is to
develop the courage to not let yourself off the hook quickly.
Instead of convincing yourself that you tried your best and
quickly getting back to business, it is important to stay on that
hook for a while. You need to suffer some anguish and discomfort so you can take the time to understand what really
went wrong. While your mind wants to protect itself from the
pain of dissonance with self-justification, your soul may be
begging you to own up and apologize. When you develop the
courage to confront yourself, you can reduce the dissonance
and confess your mistakes in a vulnerable, authentic fashion.

But how do we know that fallibility, vulnerability, and
transparency lead to positive outcomes for us and our organizations? Let's examine the evidence.

"I'm Sorry about the Rain"

Imagine this experiment: Complete strangers are brought
into a research laboratory and divided into pairs. Each pair
is assigned to a separate room and tasked with asking each
other specific questions for forty-five minutes. Now, imagine two different scenarios. In the first, the people in each
room discuss superficial, small-talk types of questions such
as "What is your favorite holiday?" and "What is your favorite

TV show?" In the second scenario, the pairs have to address a set of questions known as "the thirty-six questions of love": these are deep questions that force the individuals to show vulnerability to each other. Examples of these heavy questions include, "What is the role of love in your life?" "When was the last time you cried in front of someone else?" and "Of all the people in your family, whose death would you find the most disturbing?"

The researchers discovered that participants who were in the second scenario formed much deeper bonds with each other than those in the first. In fact, many developed long-lasting friendships, and even romantic relationships in a few cases. Astonishingly, when asked to rate the closeness of the bonds they formed with their partners, some participants in the second scenario judged it to be at the level of the bonds they have with the closest person in their lives. What this research tells us is that sharing vulnerability, even for forty-five minutes, can help people develop unusually deep connections with each other. That is why vulnerability is imperative for you if you are serious about forming close relations with your team members.

One of the tools that my colleagues at MEDI and I use when we are coaching a newly formed team is the Lifeline activity. At a team kick-off meeting, every member gets a sheet of flip chart paper. We then ask them to plot five significant personal and professional life events that brought them to this point of their career as leaders. It is amazing to observe how a group of people who barely knew each other at the beginning of the meeting can become so close after some vulnerability is shared. When people share important events from their childhoods (such as growing up as an orphan) or from their adult lives (such as losing a spouse), they express a rare vulnerability that is usually reciprocated by others and that plants the seeds for trust and deep connections.

In a study conducted in schools in New Zealand, educational leaders were asked to identify an existing concern they had with a team member. When prompted, they identified what their own contribution to the concern was. For example, some said that they hadn't done anything to resolve the complaint; that they acted in ways that were not sufficient to resolve it; or that they did not clearly communicate their concern to the other person. The leaders were then asked to audio-record a conversation about their concern with the same team member who was the subject of their concern. If the leader was willing to be vulnerable in the conversation and to disclose their contribution to the concern, the other person was more willing to talk about the concern and what they perceived to be their role in it. "These conversations appeared to be shaped by an open-minded stance by the leader and seemed to prompt an open discussion of the concern, its causes and possible solution," the researchers explained.

When you communicate your vulnerability, you help create an environment of trust in which your team members are more comfortable with openly discussing mistakes and failures. As you recall from Chapter 2, we referred to this environment as one with "psychological safety." It is well documented that leaders who act in this way create trust and better relations with their team members, which results in those team members offering more advice to the leader and showing more loyalty and engagement towards their organizations.

What is it about apologies and owning up that creates trust and better relations? In an experiment conducted at a train station on a rainy day, a researcher approached random passengers and asked if they could borrow a phone to make an emergency call. Not surprisingly, only a small number of the participants (9 percent) lent their phones to this complete stranger. However, when the researcher added an apology—"I'm sorry about the rain. Can I borrow your cell phone?"—the percentage of people who agreed to lend their phones jumped to an astounding 47 percent. Even a superficial apology for an unrelated issue such as the weather sends a signal to the other person that this is a safe place to connect and they can trust you.

In a related study, the researchers asked people to read a scenario in which a pedestrian is injured by a speeding bicyclist. They were then told to imagine that they were the injured pedestrian and to negotiate a settlement with the bicyclist. The participants were divided into three scenarios. In the first one, the bicyclist offers no apology. In the second one, the bicyclist offers a sympathetic apology: "I am sorry that you were hurt. I really hope that you feel better." And in the third scenario, the bicyclist offers a responsibility-accepting apology: "I am so sorry that you were hurt; the accident was all my fault. I was going too fast and not paying attention." The participants who were in the third group and who received the responsibility-accepting apology evaluated the bicyclist more positively and were more likely to forgive them and to accept a reasonable settlement. It is clear that when you are humble enough to apologize and own up to your part in a mistake, you will be better liked and more trusted by others, which inevitably leads to better outcomes.

One of the fundamental ways for leaders to create strong organizational cultures is to share vulnerability. In his remarkable book *The Culture Code*, journalist Dan Coyle shows that when group members communicate in a humble way to each other and admit their weaknesses, they share vulnerability in moments of trust and cooperation and unlock the group's potential to perform. An interesting point he makes is that, unlike what most assume, vulnerability has to be there first, and then trust is developed, not the other way around. First, we need to jump, and then solid ground will appear. We can't wait for solid ground to appear so we can jump. That explains the discomfort that pushes most leaders to avoid vulnerability. The Navy SEALs use a powerful tool to get over this discomfort: the After Action Review (AAR), a meeting held among team members after every mission to discuss what went well and what went wrong. Dave Cooper, one of the Navy SEALs interviewed by Coyle, emphasizes that leaders need to dig deep into their humility well to be able to show vulnerability during these AARs: "It's got to be safe to talk. Rank switched off, humility switched on. You're looking for that moment where people say 'I screwed that up.' In fact I'd say those are the most important four words any leader can say."

As I was researching for this book in the fall of 2020, the COVID pandemic was still raging throughout the world. This created some extreme changes that led to unprecedented stress and hardship. Leaders in all industries stepped up to emphasize the importance of vulnerability in these difficult circumstances. Gary Burnison, the CEO of Korn Ferry, a large multinational executive search firm, wrote a blog urging leaders to be more vulnerable: "This new normal has almost no parallel... and it's not a time for individual heroism," he said. "No one has all the answers (and if they tell you they do, run the other way). Vulnerability rules." Similarly, Janice Kaffer, the healthcare CEO we met earlier, realized how important it was to share her vulnerability with her staff while empathizing with what they were going through as front-line employees. She posted on her LinkedIn page, "Face it head on.

Talk about how hard and exhausting this is—not just for them but for you too. Vulnerability from leaders at times like this—demonstrating that we are figuring it all out too—is a strong signal that this fatigue isn't abnormal & it's ok to talk about."

While the common belief is that leaders under crises should show complete control and self-assuredness, we are learning more and more that the leaders who are navigating the current challenges effectively are actually those who admit that they don't have all the answers and who model that behavior for everyone around them. They accept that they don't know, but they quickly develop a plan to find out and to lead their organizations with vulnerability and competence. However, as we will show in the next section, there are some exceptions to the appropriateness of showing vulnerability.

Balance

Despite the overwhelming evidence about the importance of fallibility, vulnerability, and transparency for success, it is not always black and white in the world of leadership. What are the possible situations where disclosing weaknesses at work may not be as beneficial? In a study conducted among undergraduate students, participants were paired with a collaborator—who was in fact a member of the research team—to help them complete a task through computer text messages. In some situations, participants were told that the collaborator was a fellow student (i.e., a peer). In others, they were told that the collaborator had an advanced degree from a more elite college, thus signaling someone of higher status. The collaborators in both situations voluntarily shared some weaknesses about themselves in the course of the task completion. For example, "I'm on academic probation and I will have to leave if I can't improve my grades," "I'm overweight and I need to lose thirty pounds," or "I'm seeing a therapist."

When the person making the vulnerable admission was supposedly a peer, their statement had no effect on their status, influence, or relationship with the participant. However, when the person making the vulnerable admission was supposed to be someone of higher status, the participants were less likely to act on the collaborator's suggestions, appeared to like them less, and did not want to stay in touch with them after the study. The authors concluded that self-disclosure, when done by a higher status co-worker, may result in more harm than good for the relationship. They highlighted an important irony of self-disclosure: "Although higher status individuals may disclose information about their weaknesses to a co-worker in order to reduce the social distance between them and foster a better working relationship, their disclosure may have exactly the opposite effect."

This research clearly shows that in a new relationship where you haven't yet earned any status or credibility, sharing your vulnerability by admitting weaknesses may not always be the best idea. In her insightful article on the authenticity paradox in *Harvard Business Review*, Herminia Ibarra of the London Business School tells the story of a recently promoted healthcare manager named Cynthia. Cynthia's promotion increased her span of control by tenfold and expanded the range of areas that she oversees. As a result, she felt a bit unsure about herself as she was making this large leap. Because she believed in transparent leadership, Cynthia decided the best approach was to bare her soul to her new team members. "I want to do this job," she said, "but it's scary, and I need your help." Ibarra explains that Cynthia's candor with her employees actually ended up backfiring. While they were looking for someone to take charge with confidence, she actually lost her credibility by sharing her anxieties so early on. This example shows that you have to earn the right to be vulnerable and authentic. You have to prove yourself first with competence and results, then you can start bringing more and more of yourself to work to share with the team. Initially at least, you have to conform to others' expectations and to the culture of the organization. Once you have established enough legitimacy and status, then you can judiciously start sharing some of your insecurities.

How do you balance vulnerability and authenticity with being perceived as a strong leader? Picture this situation: You are being asked by your corporate bosses to enact some significant changes with your team. You may mistakenly think that you are being vulnerable and authentic by saying to your team members, "Changes are coming hard and fast, and I'm really falling apart too. I don't know what to do either. I'm not the enemy here, it's corporate who is forcing this on us." In fact, though, what the team members hear is that you want them to feel sorry for you, that you are scared, and that you do not want to take on any accountability. As a strong, humbitious leader, on the other hand, you will approach the situation differently. You will say: "Changes are coming hard and fast, and I know there is a lot of anxiety—I'm feeling it too, and it's hard. That's why I want us to discuss today how we will manage the changes and what support I need to provide to you." This sends a message of empathy to your team members, but it also tells them you are brave enough to lead them through the difficult times, and you take your responsibility as a leader seriously as you hold yourself accountable for navigating the changes successfully.

The take-home lesson is that vulnerability and authenticity are not synonymous with weakness or oversharing, and they have to be complemented with competence and credibility. You need to understand the delicate balance required in bringing different segments of your authentic self to different situations and people while maintaining your poise and executive presence. You can play different roles without being fake, and you can show vulnerability while still earning the respect and confidence of your followers.

What Next?

To sum it up, fallibility, vulnerability, and transparency are vital for you as a humbitious leader. To start working on these qualities, consider the following behaviors:

- Avoid seeking perfection, and remember that you are human.

- Work on bringing your whole self to work without oversharing.

- Apologize and take ownership for your mistakes.

- Build your credibility and status first, and then, when appropriate, share your weaknesses and insecurities.

- Admit to not knowing what the right answer is, but then use your competence and team to develop a plan to find out.

These behaviors will help you show up as a strong, authentic leader. What behaviors do you need to develop to demonstrate that you are open-minded and teachable? We will look at this in Part 3 as we move up to humility in relation to others.

three

Humble Leadership in Relation to Others

7

Open-Mindedness

I don't divide the world into the weak and the strong,
or the successes and the failures. I divide
the world into the learners and non-learners.
BENJAMIN BARBER

Hubris and Punishment

At six in the morning, with the first rays of sun appearing, the French guns started to shoot. A few seconds later, the Russian guns answered. Before too long, several thousand cannons had been discharged. Projectiles of all kinds rained on men fighting in close proximity: hails of canisters, solid iron balls weighing up to twenty pounds, and shells filled with explosives scattering fragments in all directions. On a close-by hill, an emotionless Napoleon sat, observing the battle and listening to his officers' reports, betraying no reaction. The two large and extremely well-prepared armies fought each other tooth and nail for the next thirteen hours. When nightfall finally came, the French artillery had discharged more 90,000 rounds. In this Battle of Borodino in the outskirts of Moscow, the Russians lost a staggering 45,000 men, while the French casualties were estimated at 28,000. September 7, 1812, went down in the books as a massacre: it marked the bloodiest single day in the history of warfare to that date.

While the battle itself was recorded as a French victory, hindsight showed that it was a very hollow one. Napoleon did enter Moscow a few days later, and the Russians did retreat. But the Russian tactics were working to perfection: they dragged the French armies and their allies deep into Russian territories with no plans to surrender or sign a peace treaty. Napoleon and his army stayed in Moscow for a full month, until they finally ran out of patience and food. With temperatures quickly dropping as the frigid Russian winter started, the troops had no choice but to march out of Moscow. Ragtag groups of tired, frostbitten, and malnourished men endured miserable conditions of snow, ice, and mud. Tens of thousands died of hunger and cold before they even managed to leave Russia. By the time Napoleon was back in France, a mere 20,000 of his men were alive out of the 500,000 that he had taken with him to Russia as part of the Grande Armée.

Since that fateful winter in 1812, countless historians, strategists, and leadership scholars have attempted to analyze what led to Napoleon's fatal setback in Russia. Many factors have been considered, such as poor planning, the cold weather, the enemy's military intelligence, and bad luck. But the real underlying reason, according to many experts and accounts from people who fought in the battle, was Napoleon's extreme arrogance and closed-mindedness. "Napoleon, supreme egoist that he was, ignored the significance of the omens until he and his host were completely and irrevocably committed to an undertaking that was doomed. Never did the gods punish hubris more severely," noted the Duke of Fezensac, a French officer who participated in the battle.

From the time he first started rising through the army ranks in post-revolutionary France, Napoleon had been driven by insecurity. He was extremely thin-skinned, prone to self-promotion, and needing to show strength at all times. Infatuated by Roman emperors from an early age, he copied Augustus and named himself Emperor of the French. Fueled by his desire to control Europe and build a vast empire, he amassed victory after military victory and conquered vast territories. The only power that stood between him and utter domination of the continent was Russia and its tsar, Alexander. Despite all the red flags and warnings, Napoleon's unchecked ego convinced him that the only way forward was to march to Russia and bring Alexander to his knees.

Historical accounts of the period leading to the French invasion of Russia clearly show that several senior officers strongly advised Napoleon against an attack. For example, his ambassador to the Russian Court, General Armand Louis de Caulaincourt, had heard Alexander explain his strategy for defeating Napoleon a few months before: prolong the war, refuse to sign a peace treaty, and let the cruel winter take care of the French army. Napoleon shrugged off the warnings and Alexander's prophetic plans with typical arrogance and responded, "One good battle will knock the bottoms out of... Alexander's fine resolutions. He is fickle and feeble." Napoleon's refusal to listen to advice, coupled by his unbounded confidence, ultimately led to his ill-advised decision to go to battle against the Russian Army.

When we analyze Napoleon's rise and fall, what is really alarming to note is that he never learned his lessons or owned up to his failures. A few years later, in the Battle of Waterloo, he portrayed the same overconfidence and repeated similar mistakes as he refused to listen to trusted advisers. The loss of that battle led to his final defeat and abdication. Exiled to the island of Saint Helena, he had the perfect opportunity to reflect on his mistakes and shortcomings. But instead of an honest assessment of how his hubris had contributed to his failures, the memoirs he produced while in exile show a broken but still defiant man rewriting history from his own perspective. The historian Robert Zaretsky notes, "Thanks to Napoleon's brilliant effort at reinvention, the book transformed a man who had been reviled as a bloody minded despot who had buried the French Revolution and enslaved Europe into a fair-minded constitutionalist who had saved the Revolution and liberated Europe's peoples."

The story of Napoleon clearly shows that leaders who are driven by their ego and who don't listen to others risk making decisions that lead to disaster. Humbitious leaders, on the other hand, are open to input and feedback because they are aware of what they know and what they don't know. Unlike Napoleon, you want to be intentional about listening to employees and customers because you are aware that you don't know everything and that your views may be wrong. You need to admit that you don't have all the answers, which we referred to as transparency. You also need to know what you don't know and that sometimes you may be wrong, a quality called *intellectual humility*. Moreover, you need to be willing to change your mind when the evidence shows that you are actually wrong, which demonstrates your open-mindedness. Let's continue our journey with the first step in understanding your relationship with others.

Hamrick's Rebellion

In previous chapters, we talked about the importance of self-awareness. As a humbitious leader, you understand your own strengths, but you also acknowledge your limitations. A key aspect of this is intellectual humility, which, simply put, is knowing what you know and what you don't know.

When you are intellectually humble, you are aware of the gaps in your own knowledge and you recognize your partial understanding of the issues in your organization and environment. You might know that you have some expertise in operations, for example, but that your understanding of it is not perfect. You are also aware of the intelligence and insights of your executive team members, middle managers, and front-line employees, and you do not hesitate to solicit their opinions and suggestions. When interacting with them, you are curious and display a love of learning. You engage in deep conversations, and you listen to understand. You are intentional about attending conferences, workshops, and seminars that can help deepen your knowledge, and you are an avid reader on leadership practices and industry-specific topics. You display the ultimate wisdom that Plato praised Socrates for two thousand years ago when he said, "He doesn't claim to know what he doesn't know."

How do you know how intellectually humble you are? Imagine you have been invited to participate in a social science experiment. You are asked to read a list of sixty-four historical events and names and to assess how familiar you are with them. Unbeknownst to you, there are twenty items on the list that were totally made up by the research team. For example, they created a bogus event that never took place called Hamrick's Rebellion and imagined a historical figure that never existed called Jacques Worthington. If you are low on intellectual humility, you are more likely to pretend that you are familiar with all the items—the real and the fake. That is the experiment that former Duke psychologist Samantha Deffler and her colleagues ran to determine people's tendency to over-claim on what they know. Participants who were high on intellectual humility were better able to differentiate between the real and fake news items than those who were low on intellectual humility, thus demonstrating that their beliefs about their own knowledge were more accurate.

Over the last few years, researchers who have studied intellectual humility have devised increasingly better ways to measure it and assess its benefits for people and leaders. The "General Intellectual Humility Scale," for example, asks people to rate themselves on statements such as, "I accept that my beliefs and attitudes may be wrong" and "In the face of conflicting evidence, I am open to changing my opinions." Based on this assessment, researchers can determine the characteristics of intellectually humble people and the advantages that this trait provides them in life and at work. For example, in the study just mentioned, participants were also asked to read statements on a number of political topics, such as whether same-sex marriage should be legal, what schools should teach in their core curricula, and whether the military is justified in using drone strikes. Intellectually humble people were more likely to take time to read the statements, especially if they didn't agree with them. This indicates that intellectual humility enables people to process information longer and judge it better, a skill that is necessary for you as a leader at all levels.

Similarly, in a study of college students, those who displayed intellectual humility were more open to hearing social and political views that they didn't agree with and felt they learned more when they read about opposing views. They also had a stronger motivation to learn, used different adaptive study strategies, and were more collaborative when they worked in groups. In short, the intellectually humble students were focused on learning, not on showing off their intelligence. Intelligence, as you may have heard, is like underwear. It's important that you have it, but it is not necessary that you show it off. A recent review of the expanding literature on intellectual humility concluded that, in addition to open-minded thinking, tolerance, and the ability to evaluate balanced arguments, the intellectually humble are also more grateful, empathetic, and altruistic, which are crucial traits for leaders who aspire to high performance.

"I Disagree with Myself"

In a third-grade classroom in Michigan, the children are learning about odd and even numbers. A boy named Sean raises his hand: "I was just thinking about six... It could be an odd and even number. Three things to make it and there could be two things to make it." The teacher acknowledges Sean's opinion and asks the other children what they think of his argument. She encourages them to think of the working definition of even and odd numbers that the class covered recently. A girl named Cassandra respectfully disagrees with Sean and explains that numbers have to alternate between odd and even. She tells him that six cannot be odd since it is preceded by five, an odd number.

The class proceeds to have a discussion, and then finally another girl, named Mei, walks to the board and eloquently explains that even if numbers can be made of even and odd groups, that doesn't make them even *and* odd. When he is finally convinced by the evidence being presented to him, Sean states, "I disagree with myself." He admits, "I didn't think of it that way. Thank you for bringing that up." This ten-minute educational video showing third graders discussing math principles is a perfect example of intellectual humility in action. You are probably thinking to yourself, "Why don't meetings with my team go that way?"

What this video shows us is that, under the right conditions, intellectual humility can be nurtured in classrooms and in organizations. Recent research has established that its benefits are evident even at a very young age. Judith Danovitch and her colleagues at the University of Louisville studied children aged six to eight. The children were asked to assess their own knowledge on topics such as "why fish can only live in water" or "why cars need gas." They were also asked to take a brief IQ test and then to play a computer game while having their brain activity recorded on an EEG. Some of the children rated their own knowledge more accurately and were more likely to defer to experts when they didn't know something, thus displaying signs of intellectual humility. The brain activity of these intellectually humble students showed that they spent more time thinking about their own mistakes and were more likely to know that they actually made a mistake. Not surprisingly, these students also scored higher on the intelligence test than students who were low on intellectual humility.

Similarly, other studies have shown that intellectually humble kids are more motivated to learn and tend to quiz themselves on answers to check their own understanding. Their teachers judge them to be more engaged in learning, and they generally earn better grades than non-humble kids.

But not only is intellectual humility associated with better intelligence and superior academic performance, children themselves also tend to favor the trait, even when thinking about adults. In one experiment, a group of ten- and eleven-year-olds were asked to listen to three people answering questions in different ways and to determine which person they liked more. The majority of the students preferred the person who answered questions with humility, displaying confidence about their answers but inviting and welcoming suggestions. The two people in the scenarios who were not favored by the children either answered with arrogance and were dismissive of others' beliefs, or answered with diffidence and were hesitant to give an opinion. I am not suggesting that your employees are similar to pre-teens, but there is ample evidence that most people are drawn to intellectually humble leaders.

Flip-Flopping

Intellectually humble people, because they are more willing to question their own opinions, are more tolerant and less punitive of people who change their opinions. This is an important quality for leaders to have: when you model the behavior of disagreeing with yourself as new counterevidence emerges, the people on your team feel more comfortable doing the same, and discussions become more honest, which inevitably leads to better decisions.

Unfortunately, changing your opinion is not looked upon favorably in our society. If we go back to the presidential elections of 2004, for example, the major catchphrase attack on losing candidate John Kerry was that he flip-flopped on several issues (i.e., that he said one thing and then said its opposite on issues such as the war in Iraq, the Patriot Act, or the death penalty for terrorists). This was no more evident than when Kerry tried to explain his vote on the well-known supplemental appropriation for military operations in Iraq and Afghanistan: "I actually did vote for the $87 billion, before I voted against it." Supporters of his opponent, President George W. Bush, started showing up to campaign events dressed as full-sized John Kerry flip-flops. Among many other factors, these flip-flopping accusations were a major reason why Kerry lost the election.

Why do we believe that changing our stance on an issue after getting new information is bad? The root cause of this belief, some experts argue, is a general lack of intellectual humility in our society. People who are low on intellectual humility, studies show, are more likely to believe that politicians who changed their attitudes were "flip-flopping," whereas those who display high intellectual humility do not share those beliefs. It is true that politicians—on both sides of the aisle—often have disingenuous motives in changing their opinions, such as to attract support or votes. However, we would all benefit from more positively viewing people who change their minds based on new evidence.

The belief that we know more than we actually do, and the lack of understanding of how limited our knowledge can be, is a phenomenon often referred to as the *illusion of knowledge*. In his notable recent book *The Death of Expertise*, Thomas Nichols of the U.S. Naval War College provides some insight about the prevalence of this illusion. He notes that the openness of the internet and the 24-hour cable news cycle are exposing us to more knowledge than we've ever had before. This knowledge, however, is fueling a narcissistic trend in which we start feeling like experts on every possible topic. He explains: "We've all met them, they're our co-workers, our friends, our family members... But they all have one thing in common: They are ordinary people who believe they are actually troves of knowledge. Convinced that they are more informed than the experts, more broadly knowledgeable than the professors, and more insightful than the gullible masses, they are the explainers who are more than happy to enlighten the rest of us about everything from the history of imperialism to the dangers of vaccines."

Since many of us fall into this illusion of knowledge, it is no surprise that we want the leaders who represent us to appear to know everything as well. Even when they don't have all the answers, we *want* them to pretend to be confident and decisive. When we don't vote for the politician whom we labeled a flip-flopper, we are choosing to support the stubborn, non-humble candidate who never changes their mind despite the facts at their disposal. In short, we are keeping the intellectually humble out of leadership positions. In a post on *The Conversation*, psychology professor Frank T. McAndrew writes that "while there has probably never been an excess of intellectual humility in Washington, D.C., it's rarely been as nakedly apparent as it is today."

The danger of this trend becomes even more significant when you bring these same beliefs to your workplace. Your biases may be leading you to hire and promote intellectually arrogant individuals as you pass over the intellectually humble ones. However, as a humbitious leader, you have the choice and ability to change your mindset and behaviors. When someone on your team weighs the evidence and takes the time to make a decision, you need to applaud them rather than call them indecisive or mock their inability to "go with their gut." If they are genuinely curious to find out why others have different viewpoints, you should celebrate their collaborative skills rather than penalize them for being "wishy-washy." The research evidence we have presented so far strongly suggests that the more intellectually humble you and your team are, the better your outcomes will be.

"I Could Be Wrong, But . . ."

Intellectual humility and open-mindedness are two sides of the same coin. But what does open-mindedness mean? "The test of open-mindedness is . . . whether or not we are prepared to entertain doubts about our views," explains William Hare of Dalhousie University. Open-mindedness is an attitude towards your beliefs that consists of a genuine readiness to revise them when called for. Let me stress, though, that being open-minded is not about being indecisive. As a leader, you can have strong convictions and still be open-minded. For example, you may say things such as:

- "I don't think this is the right strategy for our organization, but I will keep an open mind."

- "Vanessa is confident that the new product will never be as good as the old product. But she's an open-minded person and is willing to be proved wrong."

- "Andre believes that Obamacare was a good policy but is open to reconsidering his views based on the actual outcomes of the program."

These types of remarks reveal that open-mindedness does not mean a lack of commitment to a certain view. It just means a willingness to subject one's view to further review and scrutiny.

When Ben Franklin decided to work hard on attaining humility (as we saw in Chapter 5), he became very intentional about the words that he used in his conversations. He explained his thinking process: "I forbid myself... the use of every word or expression in the language that imported a fixed opinion, such as certainly, undoubtedly, etc., and I adopted, instead of them, I conceive, I apprehend, or I imagine a thing to be so or so, or it so appears to me at present." Franklin aimed to start his sentences with, "I could be wrong, but..." in order to prime himself to be open-minded to change his opinion. Again, this does not make you a wimpy leader, it just sends the message that you are always open to learning new perspectives.

In addition to the words you use, what traits and behaviors can you follow to be more open-minded? In the rest of this chapter, we will discuss how to display curiosity, show empathy, ask good questions, listen to understand, model learning and growth, and even encourage dissent.

Let us start with curiosity. When examining curiosity within the context of human interactions, it is important to remember the origin of the word itself. Curiosity comes from the Latin *cura*, which means care or concern. That root implies that you can't be curious about someone unless you care about them. In long-term relationships, for example, some couples often complain that they feel unheard and uncared for. What is typically happening is that the other person has lost their curiosity in them.

Unfortunately, recent research has shown that this may also be happening in many workplaces: leaders only pretend to care, and their employees do not believe it. In a large survey of C-suite executives and employees, 83 percent of the leaders claimed that curiosity is encouraged in their organizations, but only 52 percent of the followers agreed. As a humbitious leader, when you have genuine curiosity, you display a sincere willingness to learn. You enter every interaction or conversation with the mindset that you want to understand the other point of view, even if you don't have to agree with it. You model the avid curiosity that Einstein promoted when he famously said, "I have no special talents, I am only passionately curious." And by doing the same, you give your team members the permission to be curious themselves, which can only lead to better decisions and higher performance.

A natural byproduct of curiosity is asking good questions that are genuine attempts to learn. But that is much easier said than done. The evidence shows that 40 percent of our questions are statements in disguise, 40 percent are masked judgments, and only 20 percent are sincere efforts to gain additional information. One of the most important tools of humbitious leadership is to ask questions that are motivated by a sincere desire to learn. A tool I have learned for assessing the leadership style of a given individual in my coaching is to observe them in meetings and to count the number of good questions they ask in relation to the number of statements they make. A high questions-to-statements ratio is a clear indicator of humbitiousness.

Former MIT organizational development professor Edgar Schein refers to this approach as humble inquiry. He describes it as "the fine art of drawing someone out, of asking questions to which you don't already have the answer, of building a relationship based on curiosity and interest in the other person." He explains that asking empowers others and builds trust, while telling puts them down and builds dependence. The secret is to ask questions without making any assumptions about what the other person knows or needs. You need to access your own ignorance, clear your mind, and ask questions in the least biased and threatening way. For example, if a colleague is having obvious challenges with their leadership approach, instead of asking, "Have you considered getting help from someone?" consider asking, "What are you doing about your leadership development?" The first question is threatening and likely to trigger defensiveness, while the second comes from a place of curiosity and care.

As you master the art of asking curious questions, you start behaving more like a coach and less like an advisor. Coaching is about staying curious a little longer, and not rushing to give advice. While advice is definitely helpful in some situations, so often we offer it to others even if they didn't ask for it or don't need it. In his outstanding book *The Coaching Habit* and its sequel, *The Advice Trap*, leadership coach Michael Bungay Stanier has a deceptively simple suggestion for leaders: ask more questions and give less advice. To do this, you have to first "tame your advice monster"—this is what has convinced you that you were hired to have the right answers, and that if you don't, then you have failed at your job. An important aspect of this taming process is to develop the humility to "know your voice isn't the only voice, and maybe not the best voice." Bungay Stanier suggests that some of the best questions for a leader to ask when a team member comes to them are, "What's on your mind?" "And what else?" "What is the real challenge for you here?" "What do you want?" and then, finally, "How can I help?" When you adopt this approach, you start adding value by empowering others, you support them in making their own choices rather than making choices for them, and you teach them to lead, rather than doing all the leading yourself.

Switch from Selfie Mode

Being curious and asking good questions is only the start for becoming more open-minded. What is even more important is to listen after you have asked those good questions. Similar to the ratio of questions to statements, the ratio of listening to talking is another important indicator of humbitious leadership. When you are in a conversation or a meeting, your aim should be to decrease your talking time and increase your listening time. Think of it like a sports analyst who is tracking ball possession during a soccer game. As a humbitious leader, you don't want to hog the ball all the time, as the water carriers clearly showed us in Chapter 2.

But I am great listener, you may be thinking. You're not alone in having that thought. Just as most people believe they are excellent drivers, most people also believe they are excellent listeners. In both situations, they are most likely wrong, because what we think great listening is all about is very different from what it actually is. This is not about fake listening, where you nod your head and say "uh-huh" every few minutes. This is about true empathetic listening.

What does that look like? If you are in a conversation with a colleague who is a really good empathetic listener, here is what you will see. They don't stay silent; rather, they ask you curious questions that promote insight. They don't focus on finding errors in your reasoning or logic; rather, they support your points of view and convey confidence in them when appropriate. And then, only after they have listened long enough to gain adequate understanding, they will politely ask your permission to give you some advice.

These behaviors of great listening are based on solid research. Do you remember organizational researchers Jack Zenger and Joe Folkman from Chapter 2? They studied more than 3,000 participants in a coaching development program and compared the top 5 percent of listeners (as judged by other coaches) with the average listeners. Their main conclusion was that great listeners do not act like a sponge that absorbs others' thoughts and energy, as is popularly thought. Great listeners actually act like a trampoline that energizes, amplifies, and clarifies others' thoughts and insights.

While this research shows the importance of being actively engaged in the conversation and offering ideas and suggestions, it is equally important for a humbitious leader to practice support responses and to stay away from shift responses. When you give a support response, you encourage the other person to elaborate on their point so you can better understand what they are saying. When you engage in a shift response, you direct the attention from the other person to yourself by switching the topic to your own knowledge and experience.

Let me illustrate. A colleague pops into your office looking all tired. He exclaims: "I'm so busy this month." A shift response from you would sound like this: "Me too, I'm totally overwhelmed. In addition to all the projects that I'm working on, my boss just gave me two new assignments yesterday. How I am supposed to finish it all while taking care of my sick father and with a newborn at home?" Instead of listening to his concern, you have shifted the conversation towards yourself and your own concerns. Compare and contrast that with a support response: "Oh, you're very busy? What do you have to get done?" This response automatically shines the light on the other person and gives him permission to share more with you, which may lead to you agreeing to collaborate on some projects or to helping him with delegating some other ones.

A clever analogy for shift response versus support response is to think of the conversation as taking place through the camera of your smartphone. Rather than putting it into selfie mode, where you can see only yourself, keep it in regular mode, where you exclusively see the other person. Unfortunately, most of us spend 60 percent of our conversation time in selfie mode talking about ourselves, a conduct that experts refer to as "conversational narcissism."

The bottom-line behavior for listening is that you need to listen to understand, instead of just listening to reply. In his popular book *The 7 Habits of Highly Effective People*, Stephen Covey explains the difference when he introduces the crucial habit of "seeking first to understand and then to be understood." He describes how most people listen to reply: when they are in a conversation, they are either speaking or preparing to speak. They are constantly filtering everything they hear through their own paradigms and experiences. The more you obsess about coming up with the right thing to say, the more you miss of the conversation, and the more likely it is that you will not say the right things. However, when you listen to understand, you focus only on comprehending. When the other person finishes their thoughts, you can then take a moment or two to think about whether you have something to say to them.

What if you get sidetracked by your own thoughts? Well, you can always admit it: "I'm sorry, I got distracted for a second, do you mind repeating that last point?" Trinity University president Danny Anderson, whom we met earlier, explained to me his approach to listening: "For me, a humble leader is someone who genuinely listens to others. I may not agree or take the advice, but I listen. I don't have to respond to what people tell me right away; I don't show any reaction. I say, 'Let me have time to think about it.' Or, I say, 'Let me make sure I understood you correctly,' or, 'My assumption is …' Then, the other person says to themselves, 'Wow, this person is really listening to me.'" To listen with empathy, you have to be heavily engaged in the conversation, but without dominating it.

"It's Okay to Be a Work in Progress Here…"

When Fred Gluck started in his new role as managing director at McKinsey & Company, he was given a tricky first assignment. One day, he bumped into Marvin Bower, the CEO. Bower asked him how his assignment was going and Gluck felt he needed to be honest. He shared that the partners working on the assignment were approaching it the wrong way. Bower listened intently to the newcomer. The following day, Gluck found a note asking him to report to Bower. He thought he was going to get fired for speaking up against his more senior colleagues. But when he got to Bower's office, he actually found him on the phone with the project leader, sharing Gluck's points and agreeing with his arguments. The team eventually decided to redesign the whole approach for the project and refused to charge the client for it.

This was just one example of an important principle that the legendary Marvin Bower promoted throughout his career. He called it the "obligation to dissent." This means that the most junior or newest member of a team is given the permission to disagree with the most senior executive in any given conversation or meeting. Another executive who worked with Bower at McKinsey explained the benefits of the principle: "If you have an obligation to dissent, then we get the best minds and we get the best outcomes. People like living in that environment. They feel valuable. People become fearless."

As a humbitious leader, you encourage others to speak their minds. You urge them to bring attention to misbehaviors or mistakes taking place throughout the organization. And you embolden them to be direct and strong-willed in their evaluations of you. In addition to the obligation to dissent, you also model for your followers how to grow. In a series of in-depth interviews with leaders, Brad Owens and David Hekman documented how this modeling results in followers believing that learning is legitimate in the workplace. "Leader humility at the most basic, fundamental level appears to involve leaders catalyzing and reinforcing mutual leader-follower development by eagerly and publicly (i.e., outwardly, explicitly, transparently) engaging in the messy process of learning and growing," they noted. As a humbitious leader, you don't just talk about the importance of learning, you transparently exemplify how to learn by listening, observing, and learning by doing, thus modeling teachability.

When followers feel like their development journey is legitimized and that "it's okay to be a work in progress here," increased psychological freedom and engagement result. At the same time, Owens and Hekman say, the leaders themselves feel increased freedom and joy. This creates an environment of dialogue and experimentation throughout the organization, which inevitably leads to learning. The advantageous outcomes of listening and open-mindedness are well documented in the literature. Studies have shown that active empathetic listening leads to better social skills in terms of the ability to initiate and remain engaged in social interactions, the tendency to be attentive to others, and the sense of tact and social adeptness. Openness results in increased learning capacity in terms of the ability to engage in learning activities that lead to positive outcomes, and to better job satisfaction. When teams are more open, they are less dogmatic in their ideas, more willing to consider different opinions, and less likely to deny conflict, which results in better overall performance.

What Next?

To sum it up, intellectual humility and open-mindedness are the starting points for humility in relation to others. As a humbitious leader, here are a few behaviors you should keep in mind:

- Encourage intellectual humility on your team by rewarding people who are brave enough to change their minds when new evidence appears.

- Train yourself to be open-minded to others' ideas and beliefs, while still having strong ideas and beliefs for yourself.

- Practice curiosity by being genuinely interested in people and conversations.

- Ask good questions that are sincere attempts to understand the other person and their point of view.

- Listen to understand in an active and empathetic way.

- Refrain from giving advice except after you have listened and if the other person specifically asks for it.

- Take notes during meetings when others are talking.

- Jump in the trenches every now and then to re-learn about your area or organization and gain new perspectives.

- Encourage and reward team members to dissent to your ideas.

- Model learning and growth to others by making self-development legitimate.

The more you realize how much you don't know and how much other people may know, the more appreciation you will develop for their talents and skills, which is the next step in your journey of understanding your relations with others.

— 8 —

Appreciation

*Humility, while starting from the assumption
that nothing is owed us and everything is a
gift and a miracle, more than all else it causes
everything to gain in value!*

MAX SCHELER

"I Wanted Them to Know It Was from Me"

"My mom was right," said Doug Conant. "When we got gifts
for the holidays, she didn't let us open them until after we
wrote a thank-you note to the person who gave them to us."
Little Doug hated writing notes, and he wasn't good at it. He
actually didn't appreciate the importance of thank-you notes
until later on in his life, after one time when he had lost his
job. As he started his search process to find a new job, his
outplacement counselor advised him to write a thank-you
note for everyone who gave him an interview or who helped
him along the way, including the receptionists and executive
assistants. Conant took the advice to heart and carried enve-
lopes and stamps with him everywhere he went. He mailed
the notes within twenty-four hours of meeting the person.

This impressed people, and he soon received an offer. He has been writing thank-you notes ever since!

In 2001, Conant was appointed as CEO of Campbell's Soup, a company that was seriously struggling. It was bleeding money right and left and employee morale was rock-bottom. In five short years, Conant and his executive team turned it around. And, by 2011, Campbell's Soup was outperforming its competitors and ranking among the best places to work in the United States. What one behavior allowed Conant to spearhead this transformation? Yes, you guessed it: thank-you notes. Every day, on the train on his way back from work, he wrote about ten to twenty notes, for a total of 30,000 notes over ten years. He made it a point to write the notes by hand so that employees knew it wasn't some assistant who had copied and pasted a generic form letter. "I wanted them to know it was from me, that I was personally paying attention," he explained.

Conant clarifies that the notes were not gratuitous, "have-a-nice-day" type of messages. They were specific and they acknowledged each employee's efforts in advancing the company and its goals. With the help of his assistant, he scoured the company's portal every day for up to an hour looking for an opportunity to catch people doing something right. He wanted them to know that he appreciated their efforts. The employees loved receiving the notes. Anywhere he went in the company, he found the handwritten notes framed in employee cubicles or posted on bulletin boards. "What I found is, the more I say, 'Thank you for a job well done,' the more engaged the people I work with become; the more they celebrate the contributions of their peers," he said.

In addition to the notes, Conant created numerous touch-points to connect with his people. For example, every five weeks, he invited twenty employees from all levels to lunch. On some days, he put his sneakers on and walked around the Campbell's campus, thanking every employee he encountered and asking them, "How can I help?"

In 2009, Conant was in a dangerous car accident. As he was recovering after surgery in the hospital, he started receiving some notes from his employees. First it was just a dozen, then a hundred, and then the notes started coming in thousands. Many were from employees he had never personally met, but who were very grateful for having received a note from him in the past. They wanted to wish him well during this difficult time in his life. "As my wife and I sat and read them in the hospital room, I could feel them helping to speed my recovery," he explained. "The blessings of their notes reminded me that the more supportive feedback you give to others, the more you may very well receive in return." When Conant finally retired from Campbell's Soup, his employees made an eight-minute video to thank him for his thank-you notes. The video showed how much his employees appreciated his leadership style—one that was characterized by being "tough-minded on standards and tender-hearted on people." Later, in an interview, he challenged his fellow leaders with this: "What will your video say?"

Doug Conant understood the power of thank-you notes in reinforcing good behaviors. By feeling grateful for his employees' contributions and expressing that gratitude in writing, he demonstrated one of the most important behaviors for a humbitious leader: appreciating others' efforts and talents. Let us now build on the previous building blocks of humility, explore the importance of appreciation and recognition, and discuss the specific behaviors that you can adopt to express your appreciation to your team.

As Gratitude Goes, Humility Goes

Before we get to appreciation, we have to start in a deeper place: gratitude. Gratitude is the emotion of being thankful for the gifts and blessings you have in your life and for the good things others may have done for you. "What unifies expressions of gratitude is the receipt of something one desires that comes at a cost to someone else," writes David DeSteno in his notable book *Emotional Success*. He explains that while most people believe gratitude is a passive emotion that is focused on the past, the latest research actually shows that gratitude prepares people to become more cooperative, which makes it an extremely active emotion that influences future decisions.

But gratitude by itself is not enough. The novelist Gladys B. Stern was right when she noted that "silent gratitude isn't much use to anyone." You have to express the feeling to others by showing them that you are thankful through your words and actions. While gratitude is a feeling, appreciation and recognition require action. This difference between feeling and action may be a major reason why there is a significant gap between how much managers say they appreciate employees and how much employees feel appreciated by their managers. Recent research has shown that while 88 percent of CEOs believe their employees would give them high marks for leading with gratitude, only 37 percent of employees are satisfied with the level of gratitude expressed in their workplaces.

There is also an essential difference between appreciation and recognition, even though we tend to use these two terms interchangeably. Author Mike Robbins notes that recognition is about giving positive feedback, in both formal and informal ways, when someone has done something good for you. Appreciation, on the other hand, is about acknowledging the other person's inherent value, regardless of their actions. In short, recognition is about what people do, appreciation is about who they are.

What is the connection between gratitude, appreciation, recognition, and humility? A review of Chinese and Western perspectives shows that an "attitude of gratitude" is an integral part of humble leadership. As a humbitious leader, not only do you demonstrate a deep knowledge of yourself and your limitations, you also have the ability to set yourself aside sufficiently in order to recognize the value of others' contributions. Similarly, appreciation—affirming others' value as human beings—is one of the most important competencies of humble leadership. These conceptual views are strongly supported by the research. Jim Collins explains that one of the main behaviors that humble and fierce leaders engaged in when transforming their organization from good to great was a practice called "the window and the mirror." When they achieved success, Level 5 leaders looked out of the window and acknowledged and appreciated their followers' contributions and efforts. However, when things went wrong, they looked themselves in the mirror and owned up to their role in the mistake.

In a series of studies conducted at Princeton and the University of California, researchers instructed some participants to write a letter of gratitude to someone who had been kind to them. Other participants were asked to write a gratitude diary over a period of fourteen days. The researchers rated the participants' self-focus and other-focus, a measure of their humility. The findings revealed that writing the letter and the diary led to higher humility, and that humility predicted feeling more grateful after writing the letter and the diary. As people feel more grateful, they tend to focus less on themselves and more on others. The researchers concluded that there is a "mutually reinforcing relationship between humility and gratitude."

The Power of Thank You

April 8, 2019

Dear Amer,

Thank you for making time to present in the Dallas Trinity on Tour.

It was a pleasure to see you in action. You are engaging as a presenter and knowledgeable as a scholar. That's a powerful combination. Thank you!

Best Wishes,

Danny

I can't describe the astonishment and delight that I felt when I received this letter. I had agreed to take the short flight from San Antonio to Dallas to spend a day with our university's alumni association and to give presentations on leadership traits and behaviors to the graduates. Danny, aka President Anderson, was in the audience. Being the humbitious leader that he is, he wanted to express his recognition. Never before had I received a handwritten note from the president of the university. I framed it and I still have it in my office.

A few months later, as I started working on this book, I reached out to Dr. Anderson by email to request a short meeting to ask him a few questions about his leadership style. Within a few hours, the answer came back: "It would be an honor to participate in your project and support your work in any way that I can." In fact, he suggested that, in addition to meeting to answer my questions in his office, we have lunch on a later date to discuss leadership and coaching in general. How amazing is that! He is the president of the university with a packed schedule.

A few days later, I showed up at Dr. Anderson's office, where he greeted me with his kind smile. He graciously and articulately answered my questions (you have seen his quotes throughout the book). But the one topic that I most wanted to ask him about was his practice of writing thank-you notes. "I try to write as many as I can. I write them for situations when people have gone out of their way, when they connect with the mission," Dr. Anderson explained. "You gain so much by catching people in the act of doing good things; lots of energy is generated." I was curious to know how he actually wrote them: What did he think about? Did he follow certain steps? "When I am writing them, I try not to follow a formula," he clarified. "I genuinely try to imagine the face of the person; I think of what they have done that I am grateful for; I try to feel like every note is the only note that I have ever written."

Handwritten thank-you notes are one of the most powerful tools in a leader's toolbox to express gratitude, as we saw earlier with the Campbell's Soup CEO. But do they have to be *handwritten*? A short while ago, I was asked this same question. I was giving a talk to a group of healthcare leaders. After I discussed thank-you notes, a young manager raised her hand and asked, "I have a lot of young people on my team. I just send them texts to thank them. It is a very fast, 'Thnx!' and this way I make sure I don't forget to thank them later. Isn't that enough?" I explained that sending a text message to express gratitude is definitely better than not expressing it at all. Then I asked: "How many text messages do you think a young team member gets per day, between personal and work messages?" She said, "Oh, I don't know, maybe a 100 or 150 at least!" I probed further: "How many handwritten thank-you notes do you think they receive per year?" She was taken aback by the question. She thought it about it for a moment, then said, "I personally only get one per year, from my grandma after Christmas!"

And that is the point. Electronic thank-you notes may be more efficient, but they can get lost in the shuffle. When you send a handwritten note, it stands out as something special; it sends the message that you have taken time from your busy day because what the other person did mattered. The receiver also has something tangible that they can look at and show to others. One of the best practices followed in the healthcare industry is the habit of sending thank-you notes to an employee's home address. Imagine the surprise and joy when a team member is home and receives an envelope from their boss or the CEO. They open it next to their family and read it aloud. Their spouse and children finally understand that all that sacrifice and hard work is appreciated.

One interesting thing to note is that the benefits of expressing gratitude are not only limited to the person receiving it. You—the sender—get some significant benefits too. Study participants who were asked to write three letters of gratitude to others over a three-week period reported feeling more happiness and life satisfaction and fewer depressive symptoms. Similarly, students and employees in another study who wrote letters of gratitude to others were more likely to engage in positive behaviors that led to improvements in their kindness, health, or work. Start the habit of writing thank-you notes and you will see immediate benefits for your team and for yourself.

Proactive Appreciation

In addition to thank-you notes, there are other behaviors that can help you express your appreciation and recognition to others. A smart approach is to be proactive rather than reactive. When the toy company Mattel was losing almost a million dollars every day, Robert Eckert was appointed as CEO to lead the turnaround. In his first day on the job, he called for a town hall meeting in the company's cafeteria. He humbly and confidently addressed the employees: "I know how this works. We will turn things around, and because I'm the new, outsider CEO, I'll get a lot of the credit. But I know who's really going to deserve the thanks—all of you. I appreciate what you're about to accomplish." Eckert set the tone in proactively acknowledging the employees' efforts, thus resulting in them feeling valued. From then on, he set aside time each week to acknowledge good work. When he sent an email to a certain employee to praise him, he remembered to cc his boss. "Don't tell me. Tell my boss" is something he had learned from his employees in the past. He wrote handwritten thank-you notes. He criticized in private and praised in public, using timely and specific words. As a result, he created a culture of gratitude that was "a game changer for sustainably better performance." It is no surprise that Eckert and his employees executed the Mattel turnaround perfectly.

As a humbitious leader, you ought to make it a habit to express your appreciation to others. You can start by touching base with your team early and often. Stop by their offices or cubicles daily to say "good morning" and to listen when they share how their kids are doing in sports or the state of their parents' health. Make it a point to make the rounds on employees who work in different buildings or sites. A highly effective approach followed by numerous hospital leaders is called "rounding for outcomes," where you block regular time on your schedule to grab your clipboard and visit your various areas. When you encounter one of your direct reports, you start by asking about their families or their weekend plans. You then proceed to ask about possible wins that their team may have witnessed recently. And then you ask: "Is there anyone you would like to recognize? Is there someone on your team going above and beyond? I would like to send them a thank-you note." You write down everything you hear, and then you follow up. Your employees will see your rounding on them in this fashion as a breath of fresh air and a radical change from the old-fashioned approach, where the only time their manager came to talk to them was when they were in trouble.

One of the behaviors that renowned power expert Dacher Keltner advises leaders to adopt in order to remain humble and avoid succumbing to the corrupting effect of power is to express gratitude with team members using appropriate touching to celebrate successes. A fascinating study done among NBA teams provides support for this approach: teams whose players touched each other more, through pats on the back, fist bumps, or high fives, after scoring points early in the season were more likely to achieve success later on. This is an approach that may better fit athletic teams or those that are predominantly made up of males. When applied in the workplace, it is vital for you to get permission from all team members and to make sure they feel comfortable getting touched before engaging in this kind of gratitude behavior.

It is also important to note that not all expressions of gratitude are equally effective. When we thank another person, we often focus on how their help has benefited us and how it has made us feel. For example, we say, "Thank you for handling this project, it allowed me to focus on the other projects I have on my plate," or "Your analyses made me look good in front of my boss." However, the research shows that when we make gratitude all about us, we may reduce its potential benefits to the other person. Instead of focusing on self-benefit, consider praising the other person and focusing on their behaviors. For example, you could say something like, "Thank you for handling this project, it shows how responsible you are," or "Your analyses clearly show that you are able to go into the weeds while keeping the big picture in mind," or "You are really good at going out of your way to collaborate with others." When you replace self-benefit expressions of gratitude with other-praising ones, the other person becomes more responsive and experiences more positive emotions, such as inspiration, pride, and even love.

Another common mistake that some leaders fall into when attempting to express appreciation or recognition is to use the same approach with everyone. It is important that you reward your employees and recognize them according to what they value. Say you are on your way back from a business trip, and you want to recognize an executive assistant who has been pulling long hours recently to successfully manage your schedule. If they are a voracious reader and have shared some of their favorite authors with you, you could grab a book you think they might like. But if they are an avid sports fan rather than an avid reader, then a scarf or cap of their favorite team (not yours!) might be the better approach. You want to make sure that your gratitude expression is not hollow.

Similarly, make sure that you are rewarding the high performers, rather than everyone on the team. There is nothing more demoralizing for a high performer than to receive a thank-you note from the boss and then to notice a similar note on the desk of the lazy employee who everyone knows isn't pulling their own weight. So when is a thank-you note appropriate? Obviously, when someone goes above and beyond their job responsibilities, they are well-deserving of your gratitude. But you can also focus your gratitude on employees who best exemplify the company's values. For example, if one of your values is collaboration and a team member has come in two weekends in a row to help people on another team, you can explicitly thank them for modeling that value to others. Just make sure that your sources about praiseworthy behaviors are reliable, and that you are not forgetting the unsung heroes whose actions don't get a lot of attention.

Bravo!

Let's take a deeper dive into the research on gratitude, appreciation, and recognition. As a humbitious leader, when you make it a habit to count your blessings and periodically reflect on what you are grateful for, your overall wellbeing and happiness improves. "Gratitude promotes the savoring of positive life experiences and situations so that maximum satisfaction and enjoyment are distilled from one's circumstances," concluded Sonja Lyubomirsky and her co-authors from their research examining the connection between gratitude and happiness. Similarly, extensive research conducted by gratitude expert Robert Emmons has shown significant physical, psychological, and social benefits of feeling grateful, such as a stronger immune system, more positive emotions, and feeling more connected to others.

When you receive help from others and feel gratitude towards them, you are then more likely to provide assistance to complete strangers, even if that assistance is costly for you in the short term. You become more loyal to the person who helped you, and engage in behaviors to make sure they are not feeling socially excluded—an important step in building long-term relationships that move beyond reciprocity. You develop more patience, and engage in more cooperative and less selfish behaviors.

We know by now that feeling grateful towards others is beneficial to us and to them. But what are the benefits of experiencing gratitude and appreciation from others? Professors Adam Grant and Francisca Gino recruited college students to participate in what was described as a study about writing skills and feedback. In return for a $10 reward, the participants were asked by a student to provide feedback by email on his job application cover letter (the "student" was actually one of the researchers). After the participants submitted their suggestions on the letter, they were led to believe that the study was over. Unbeknownst to them, they were randomly assigned into a control group or a gratitude group. Those in the control group received a second neutral email from the same student asking if they would voluntarily help him with another cover letter (with no additional monetary reward). The email read: "Dear [name], I just wanted to let you know that I received your feedback on my cover letter. I was wondering if you could help with a second cover letter I prepared and give me feedback on it." Those in the gratitude condition received a similar second email asking for help on another cover letter, but with the student expressing gratitude for the help he received on the first letter: "Dear [name], I just wanted to let you know that I received your feedback on my cover letter. Thank you so much! I am really grateful. I was wondering if you could help with a second cover letter I prepared and give me feedback on it." The findings showed that 66 percent of the participants who received the expression of gratitude agreed to help the student with the second letter, but only 32 percent of the participants who did not receive any gratitude agreed to the same.

The researchers then replicated the study among fundraisers at a public university. The fundraisers were similarly divided into a control group and gratitude group. Those in the control group went about their work of calling potential donors as usual. However, those in the gratitude group received a visit from the director of annual giving, where she expressed to them, "I am very grateful for your hard work. We sincerely appreciate your contributions to the university." Since all of the fundraisers received a fixed salary and were not receiving any commission, the researchers tracked the number of purely voluntary calls that they made—that is, calls that they initiated for no other reason than to help the university. The fundraisers that heard the expression of gratitude from the director made 50 percent more voluntary calls to donors than those who did not.

Both of these experiments clearly show that when you explicitly express your gratitude to your team members, they are much more likely to engage in what researchers call "pro-social behaviors." They help not only the person who asks them for additional help, but also other people and the organization more, even if they don't get anything in return for that additional help. Many leaders wonder how they can get their employees to put in more than the minimum effort and to be more engaged in their work. It is clear that expressing genuine gratitude for their efforts can go a long way to enabling people to go above and beyond.

A few years ago, LinkedIn implemented a new peer-to-peer recognition program called "Bravo!" where executives and employees at all levels could give monetary awards to each other at any point in time. The awards ranged in terms of their value, with the average award at about $135. While this is significant, the main intention was not to give a large amount of money, but to express sentiments of gratitude. The program became well received and widely adopted across the organization. A clear "pay-it-forward" pattern emerged: when an employee was recognized, they were more likely to recognize two other people in the organization. More awards also led to better retention rates and performance ratings. An employee who received four or more awards had a retention rate that was 10 percentage points higher than a peer who did not receive any awards. Similarly, an employee who received three or more awards improved their performance rating by 54 percent year over year. "The LinkedIn data shows not only the ripple effect that occurs in terms of performance, but the actual creation of praise recipients into praise providers. People are becoming happier and more engaged, and they're part of the process of making other people more positive and engaged," said Shawn Achor, the researcher who helped LinkedIn with the program. Other research has shown similar patterns of recognition leading to improved commitment and motivation and reduced turnover, as well as better team performance.

When Oprah Winfrey addressed Harvard graduates in a commencement speech, she expressed how her experiences have aligned with the research we have presented. She said, "I have to say that the single most important lesson I learned in twenty-five years talking every single day to people was that there's a common denominator in our human experience... The common denominator that I found in every single interview is we want to be validated... I heard it from President Bush. I heard it from President Obama. I've heard it from heroes and from housewives. I've heard it from victims and perpetrators of crimes. I even heard it from Beyoncé in all of her Beyoncé-ness... [We] all want to know one thing: Was that okay? Did you hear me? Do you see me? Did what I say mean anything to you?" Appreciation is undoubtedly one of the most important needs that humans have, and as a humbitious leader you have the power to help satisfy that need among your employees.

What Next?

Gratitude, appreciation, and recognition have clear personal, relational, and organizational benefits. As a humbitious leader, make it a habit to practice the following behaviors:

- Catch people in the act of doing something good.

- Give handwritten thank-you notes that are genuine, specific, and timely.

- Proactively appreciate others for who they are and for the value they bring.

- Recognize positive efforts and behaviors formally and informally.

- Check in with your team members periodically and with presence.

- Round on your direct reports and front-line employees with the purpose of uncovering wins and positive behaviors.

- Switch your expressions of thanks from self-benefit to praising others.

As you feel grateful and show appreciation towards what you have been given, you become more likely to give to others, which is the next step in your humbitiousness journey.

— 9 —

Generosity

The load, or weight, or burden of my neighbor's
glory should be laid daily on my back, a load
so heavy that only humility can carry it,
and the backs of the proud will be broken.

C.S. LEWIS

Twelve Stores Every Day

He visited up to twelve Costco stores every single day. He just showed up, with no entourage and no fanfare. He came in his regular Kirkland-brand shirt and his name badge that said "Jim." That's it, just "Jim," no title, nothing. He said hello to the employees, asked them questions, and listened to their answers. He also asked customers about their experience. Then he went back to the corporate office in Issaquah, Washington, to share what he learned with his executive team, and to design strategy based on that.

It may be hard to believe, but that is exactly what Jim Sinegal did during his fifteen years as CEO of Costco. He went to every single Costco store at least once per year. "I love to hear the cash registers ring," he joked. When he wasn't on the road, he was equally accessible. Sinegal answered his own phone, with no need for an assistant. When visitors came to the headquarters, he came out to the reception desk himself to greet them. Even his office was with no pretense, a little nook that had no door and was furnished with folding chairs.

In addition to how generous he was with his time, Sinegal was also very generous with employee compensation. A cashier at Costco could earn up to $40,000 per year after four years of service, something that was unheard of at other retailers. These wages, which were often criticized by Wall Street analysts, resulted in increased productivity and reduced turnover among Costco employees. Sinegal explained, "I don't see what's wrong with an employee earning enough to be able to buy a house or have a health plan for the family. We're trying to build a company that will be here fifty years from now."

Earlier in this book, we talked about how the Romans defined humility as "being close to the ground." Sinegal exemplified this closeness better than any other top executive through his approachability and generosity. He articulated that "arrogance is a like a cancer. It permeates the whole organization... Humility is necessary." If you want to be a humbitious leader like him, you need to be intentional about displaying genuine generosity, which is the last piece in humility in relation to others.

"I'm Not Here for Me"

The participants listen to an audio recording from a fellow student named Carl or Carol, who has recently injured their leg and is unable to attend class regularly. In the recording, Carl/Carol asks for help with lecture notes for a psychology course, without which they will not be able to continue at the university. Afterwards, the participants are asked to share how many hours per week they are willing to help Carl/Carol with their lecture notes. In this experiment, conducted by professor Jordan LaBouff and his colleagues, the participants also take a humility assessment. The results show that those who were more humble volunteered to help an average of 9.23 hours over three weeks, while those who were less humble volunteered only 5.85 hours. Moreover, humble students were more likely to help in situations where there was no social pressure to help—that is, when they were told that no one else volunteered to help.

In another study, researchers measured participant generosity and kindness in a number of different ways and tested the connection to humility. The results showed that humble people were more likely to give to charity, fill out an optional survey and mail it back, and give money to an anonymous stranger. Moreover, humble people reported greater motives to be kind to their friends and family members, to complete strangers, and even to someone who has been unkind to them in the past. The evidence is clear: humble people are generous and kind.

In the context of leadership, one of the most important aspects of humility is to realize that you are not in it for yourself or your own interests. Rather, as a humbitious, selfless leader, you are mainly motivated to generously serve others and to benefit the organization. As we have already seen, Level 5 leaders did not lead their organizations from good to great performance by focusing on their own needs. Rather, they had an unwavering commitment to the organization itself. This focus on the greater good leads to a profound realization that you need to grow and develop others' talents and skills. You find yourself telling your team members, "I need your collaboration, and I believe you would benefit greatly if you could develop your skills and strengthen your talent in this particular area—and it would also help us enormously as we pursue [our] goals." As a result, you unleash the enormous talent of others, which leads to better productivity and profitability for the organization.

Generous leaders give from their time, their energy, and their talents to help and develop others. A crucial prerequisite for you to demonstrate this type of generosity is to be able to understand others' feelings, to see things from their perspective, and to commit to helping them. This means that if you want to be a generous humbitious leader, you first need to develop your empathy and compassion. In her recent book *The Extraordinary Power of Leader Humility*, Professor Marilyn Gist defines leader humility as a "tendency to feel and display deep regard for others' dignity." Fascinating recent research has shown how intertwined these traits are even at a very young age. When compared to other children their age, one-year-olds whose parents demonstrate high levels of empathy tend to show greater concern for strangers as two-year-olds, are more able to connect to other people's emotions as four-year-olds, and act more generously towards others as six-year-olds.

Moreover, research from the field of neuroeconomics has revealed that the brains of generous people behave differently from the brains of others. When these people think about giving to others, a region in their brains called the temporoparietal junction is fired up. Scientists have discovered that this region is typically associated with empathy and thinking of others. When you intentionally take time to focus on how others are feeling, you are more likely to act in a generous way.

Numerous recent books have shown how important empathy, compassion, and kindness are for high-performing leaders. In her remarkable book *The Empathy Edge*, Maria Ross makes a strong case for empathy in organizations. She explains that a "soft skill" like empathy may be discarded in an age when algorithms and robots are taking over organizations. But she argues that this very quality, which makes you uniquely human, is exactly what you need in order to gain a competitive advantage in the current business environment. Being empathetic and compassionate does not negate your ability to make rational decisions, nor does it mean caving to demands or accepting a weak position for yourself or for your organization. Ross declares that you can be "compassionately competitive, kindly ambitious, and empathetic yet decisive." Compassion is sometimes mistaken for weakness, but nothing could be further from the truth because it actually requires the strength to have difficult conversations and the courage to make tough decisions.

Professor Jamil Zaki, in *The War for Kindness*, also maintains that empathy and kindness are crucial for leaders, and clarifies that empathy is less like a fixed trait and more like a skill that you can build and sharpen over time. "Through practice, we can grow our empathy and become kinder as a result," he explains. When you combine compassion with humility and generosity, you focus on doing good with a clear motivation of concern for others. You engage in acts of kindness that are intended to help your followers, rather than to make you look good.

Not All Givers Are Created Equal

Generosity is about putting empathy, compassion, and kindness into action. It requires you to go beyond caring for others and to engage in specific behaviors that benefit them. "Elegantly simple, yet extremely powerful, generosity can make your career," notes leadership development expert Jodi Glickman. As a leader, you may be preoccupied with organizational priorities and big-picture strategies. But being a humbitious generous leader requires you to focus also on the people right in front of you and to take the time to genuinely connect with them. In doing so, you can share your knowledge and experience. You spread your wisdom with the goal of helping others improve. "Don't let all the brilliance you've gathered over the years go to waste," advises Glickman. Make sure not only to highlight your achievements and proudest moments, but also to share your mistakes and the lessons that you learned from them.

Time is always a rare commodity for leaders, especially at the highest level. Obviously, you should be very protective of your time. But you also need to slow down so you can be unhurried in your daily interactions with others. You need to make intentional eye contact, ask how someone's family is doing, and actually listen to the answer. You need to show your team members that they are important for you, and you should act in ways that communicate to them that you consider their work and their lives significant.

Moreover, you need to stand up for your people to show them you are on their side with support and assistance. If a project is approaching its deadline, you may need to stay late in the office some evenings to help your team. If a team member is deserving but not being noticed, you ought to open the door for them, create the right circumstances, and help them achieve their goals. If you notice an intern or younger employee who is a bit shy or reserved, offer to take them with you to high-level meetings they wouldn't otherwise be involved in, or invite them to working lunches where new projects are being discussed.

How do you give to others without risking being taken advantage of and derailing your career? To address this question, let's take a deep dive into the work of my favorite organizational psychologist, Wharton professor Adam Grant.

Grant contends that there are three kinds of people in business: *givers*, *takers*, and *matchers*. *Givers* operate with the mindset that they are happy to share their time and energy with those who can benefit. They give more than they get, focus on the interest of others, and help without expecting anything in return. *Takers* assume that if they don't look out for themselves, then no one will. They put their own interests ahead of others and believe that the world is a competitive place with limited opportunities. *Matchers* will do something for others only if they are sure that they will get something in return. They strive to preserve a balance of giving and getting, and have relationships governed by an even exchange of favors. Based on research conducted in various industries, Grant's work explores who tends to succeed more at work: givers, takers, or matchers.

In one study, for example, professional engineers in California rated one another on help received and given. They were then evaluated on objective measures of performance. The findings showed that the worst-performing engineers gave more than they received. They spent a lot of time helping others, which led to them having the worst scores on the number of tasks, technical reports, and drawings completed, in addition to making many errors, missing deadlines, and wasting organizational money. However, the best-performing engineers were also givers, outperforming everyone else on the same measures. The takers and matchers tended to be middle performers.

Similar patterns were observed in a study conducted at Belgian medical schools. Students who anticipated others' needs and who loved to help others happened to score the lowest on their exams. They allocated valuable time to helping their fellow students by sharing their knowledge and their notes, but they forgot about themselves and wasted valuable studying time. However, the students who scored the highest on the same exams were also givers who did not hesitate to help others. Research conducted among salespeople in North Carolina, as well as among numerous other occupational groups, has shown comparable findings. Grant summarizes: "Generosity appear[s] to sink some employees to the bottom while propelling others to the top." What on earth is going on?

It turns out that there are two types of givers. The first type—the *pushovers*—are those who give without protecting their time or thinking about their own interests. They are typically taken advantage of by others and end up with "generosity burnout." The second type—the *effective givers*—give generously but are smart enough to protect their time and advance their own interests. What makes them different from the takers is that they achieve successes without hurting others or ignoring their needs. If you are a successful giver, everyone will root for you because they have already benefited from your generosity and good deeds in one way or another. It's easier to succeed if everybody wants you to succeed. When you don't create enemies on your way to the top, people will support you without feeling jealous.

What are some behaviors that you can adopt to become more of a successful giver? First, you need to set limits on how available you are to others so that you can avoid being taken advantage of. Make sure your "open-door" policy does not mean "open all the time."

For example, if mentoring is one of your favorite ways of expressing your generosity, make sure to reserve one day every week or every other week for meetings with your direct reports for mentoring, while dedicating the rest of your week to finishing your work and achieving your own goals. Another idea is to create specific "office hours" for drop-ins by employees from all levels in the organization. Managers and employees who are two or three levels below you in the hierarchy will feel they have access to you, but at limited times. There is strong evidence that if you know how to manage your time, you can become even more productive as you help others.

If that is still not enough to meet the demands of all the people who need mentorship and advice in your organization, try to reduce the burden on yourself by soliciting other leaders on your team to become mentors too. Grant refers to this as "scaling-up mentoring," and notes that "leaders have the unique opportunity to multiply themselves and create networks of givers." In summary, avoid being a "universal donor." You can be an effective giver only if you are fully energized. Think of it as being like your bank account: spending without putting money in eventually leads to a negative balance.

"I'd Like to Pay for the Next Customer"

Bobby Herrera, the founder and CEO of the successful HR firm Populus Group (PG), was born into an immigrant family from Mexico who traveled six months each year to different locations to work in the fields. They struggled to make ends meet. When Bobby was seventeen, he played on the high school basketball team with his younger brother. One night, on their way back from an away game, Bobby and his brother were on the team bus with the rest of the team. The driver stopped at a small restaurant so the players could get some dinner. Everyone got off the bus except for Bobby and his brother: they didn't have any money, so their mom had packed some burritos for them.

A few minutes after everyone disappeared inside the restaurant, the father of one their teammates reboarded the bus. He sat next to Bobby. He then kindly said to him: "Bobby, it would make me very happy if you would allow me to buy you boys dinner so you can join the rest of the team. No one else has to know. To thank me, you just have to do the same thing in the future for another great kid, just like you." That generous gesture had a profound impact on Bobby and changed the course of his life. Many years later, he reflected on what it meant: "That day on the bus I felt seen for the first time. Someone had not only noticed me, they had offered a great kindness and given me a purpose—to offer this same generosity to someone like myself in the future ... Didn't that imply success? Someone who could offer and make things happen for other people." He never forgot it.

Herrera became determined to change his circumstances and build something different from the life of struggle he had experienced so far. He went to college, worked hard, and later founded PG, a now $500 million business. What makes the company especially successful, according to Herrera, is that it was built on the principles of generosity and compassion. "Leadership amounts to wanting more for our people than we want from them. At PG, that means generosity and compassion is the way we work. It's the best way we know to cultivate great leaders and maintain a healthy bottom line," Herrera explains.

Bobby Herrera believes the seeds of generosity were planted in him on that evening on the team bus when he was encouraged to pay it forward to others. Paying it forward can take many different forms. For example, on a cold morning in December 2012, a customer in the drive-through of a Tim Hortons in Winnipeg offered to pay for the next customer behind them in line. That person then picked up the tab for the following car, and so on and so forth until 226 customers in total had paid it forward! The practice then spread to other drive-throughs and restaurants all over Canada and the United States. These events confirm what Bobby Herrera has known all along: receiving help can increase the willingness to be generous towards others. Recent research has supported this notion by showing that leaders can leverage the contagiousness of giving: the more you help and develop your team members, the more those team members will help and develop others, thus creating chain reactions at all levels of the organization.

Your aim as a humbitious leader should be to build a culture where generosity is the norm and giving is spread to everyone in your organization. For example, when you are mentoring a unit manager, encourage them to mentor others on their team. Be intentional about having short meetings with bursts of attention and energy that can have a lasting impact. When a new employee joins the organization, plan to stop by their desk, shake their hand, and ask questions that show interest in that employee and their success. The whole interaction may last only five minutes, but it will mean the world to them. They will always remember that the boss took the time to talk to them, and they will likely do the same themself when they become a leader.

The organizational researcher and advisor Liz Wiseman calls the types of leaders who create large networks of givers "multipliers." In contrast to selfish leaders, they are mostly focused on attracting talent and developing it, rather than on building empires for themselves. As a multiplier, you look for talent from outside and inside your organization at all levels. You actively seek to identify their innate strengths and help promote them across the organization. You shine a spotlight on them, you connect them with opportunities, and then you get out of their way as they start achieving success.

The research clearly shows that when people are part of a more empathetic group and observe generous behaviors, they tend to have more empathetic feelings and act more generously themselves. But the opposite is also true: when you act in a selfish way as a leader, your followers will behave more selfishly. When you model selfish behaviors, such as not sharing information with colleagues or ignoring email messages, you make these behaviors appear to be less shame-worthy for your followers. As we know, what gets modeled gets repeated.

The KIND Way

There are obvious organizational benefits to giving and generosity. Studies have shown that when employees are involved in opportunities for growth and development, they feel more appreciated, valued, and satisfied. Moreover, the giving behavior of the top leader in the organization is a key driver of several organizational outcomes. Professor Suzanne Peterson and her colleagues asked the CFOs of technology organizations to rate their CEOs in terms of their giving behaviors. For example, they evaluated whether "the CEO seems to care more about the organization's success than his/her own," and if "the CEO emphasizes the importance of giving back to the community." The results showed that CEOs who were more giving improved their firms' financial outcomes measured in terms of return on assets. It appeared that when CEOs are more other-focused and generous, they improve the performance of the organization by motivating and empowering their followers "to reach their full potential and feel engaged in a greater cause that benefits a wide range of stakeholders."

Daniel Lubetzky understands the importance of generosity for leaders. He is the founder of KIND, a company that makes healthy snacks, and he is also now one of the judges on the popular show *Shark Tank*. When he talked to me by phone from his office in New York City, Lubetzky shared that he learned generosity from his father, a humble man who escaped the Holocaust in Europe to start his life from scratch in Mexico. He remembered, "The best role model of humility and kindness is my father. He had those qualities in aces. His life was not about himself. He was a very good coach, he listened well. If you were to ask him a question, he would answer you with another question about you. He was in a league of his own." As an example, despite the family's limited means, Lubetzky's father consistently gave money to a blind man who used to beg on a street near their home. One day, Lubetzky noticed that the "blind" man got in a fancy car and drove away. He asked his father if he was upset to be the victim of a con artist. "I'd rather make the mistake of giving to someone who doesn't need it than run the risk of not giving a hand to someone who does," came his father's reply.

Lubetzky admits that his father was the main reason he decided to start the company and call it KIND. "His entire story… was a string of kindness. He treated everyone as an equal, whether a bank teller or the bank president." At KIND, everyone is treated equally in that they have the same compensation structure. Of course, different employees get different salaries, but whether you are just out of college or the president, there are four elements in your compensation: salary, bonus, long-term incentives in cash, and stock options, something that is not common in other organizations. The company also values small acts of kindness, such as smiling, being respectful, and not judging someone if they are having a bad day. Lubetzky also learned that from his father. "If we were at a restaurant and the waiter was grumpy, my father wouldn't get annoyed. Instead he would tell them jokes, ask them questions, and walk them through their problems. He would always try to cheer them up," he recalled.

One of the ways that the company spreads acts of kindness in the world is through their innovative #kindofawesome cards. If Lubetzky or any KIND employee notices someone doing an act of kindness, such as a passenger on the subway giving up their seat to an older person, they approach that person and give them one of these cards. The card directs the generous person to a website, where they can enter a code. The company then sends them a packet with KIND bars and another #kindofawesome card for that person to give to someone else who is engaged in a kind act. Channeling his father's ideals into his company's culture, Lubetzky has created a highly prosperous company. It is no surprise that by doing good, KIND does really well. It is one of the most successful companies in its niche in terms of sales and profitability.

It Is Satisfying

Not only can giving lead to better organizational outcomes, it can also have important benefits for the givers themselves. Research has shown that people who give more social support to others have lower blood pressure and healthier hearts than people who give less. Moreover, when people donate to charity, especially on a voluntary basis, specific pleasure-related centers in their brains are activated. Scientists have discovered that these are the same centers that light up when people actually receive money, thus indicating that giving can be as pleasurable as receiving.

These findings apply to all types of rich and poor countries. A study conducted in 136 countries revealed that people who recently made a donation to charity reported greater satisfaction with their lives. More specifically, when comparing people in countries that differ significantly in terms of income, such as Canada and Uganda, it was discovered that people report greater satisfaction after reflecting on a time when they spent money on others versus spending money on themselves, and after buying a gift for a sick child versus a gift for themselves. The authors concluded that "human beings around the world experience emotional rewards from using their financial resources to reward others."

When people feel that their giving makes a difference, they experience even greater satisfaction. Research by Professor Lara Aknin and her colleagues found that people who gave money to charity felt happier only when they gave to causes that explained how the funds are used to make a difference in the life of the recipients. In another study, participants reflected on times when they gave to others with either a positive impact or no impact at all. Those who thought about the time when their giving had a positive impact were the happiest. As a leader, you need to make sure that the givers in your organization understand the positive impact they are making on the careers of others. For example, if one of your team members spent a lot of time developing a young intern and that intern just got promoted, you need to find ways to connect the two of them again to ensure that the team member continues their generous behavior with other interns.

In other research, Michael Poulin and his colleagues wanted to understand the possible positive effects of giving on reducing mortality risks among older adults. They asked the seniors in the study whether they engaged in voluntarily helping, such as regularly driving someone to their doctor's appointment, doing their grocery shopping for them, or babysitting their kids. They also checked if the seniors had experienced a stressful event in the past twelve months. The findings showed that stressful events such as serious illnesses, burglaries, job losses, financial difficulties, or the death of a family member increased a senior's mortality risk by 30 percent. However, this applied only to individuals who did not help others. For those who consistently helped their neighbors, friends, or relatives, stress had no effect on their risk of dying. It turns out that helping others (the study did account for factors that might have affected the seniors' ability to help) had a "buffering effect" that completely eliminated the negative impact of stress.

Similar results have been reported in organizations. A longitudinal study of a formal mentoring program in an English police force found that people who mentored junior team members experienced less anxiety and felt more meaning in their jobs than people who did not engage in mentoring. In fact, some of the mentors described their interactions with their mentees as therapeutic. "Doing this lets you do something important for someone and see the results fairly quick. You are helping them. They don't always listen, but it is satisfying. More than a lot of what I have to do these days," stated a senior officer who served as a mentor.

A word of caution on giving and volunteering before we wrap up this chapter: you need to make sure that others want your help before you offer it. The research is clear that when you offer unsolicited help, it is typically not appreciated and neither you nor the receiver reap much benefit from it. Remember that what you perceive as a problem for someone else may not actually be a problem for them. Also, sometimes people prefer to solve a problem on their own in order to learn from the experience. By swooping in to solve their problem, you may be robbing them of a valuable lesson. In both cases, your help will not be valued and might even lead to a strained relationship with the receiver. So ask for permission first, and then offer your help.

What Next?

Generosity and giving are the last building blocks of humbitious leadership in relation to others. To practice these traits, here are some tips:

- Invest your time and energy into growing and developing others for their benefit and the benefit of the organization.

- Practice feeling what others are feeling, and thinking what they are thinking, so you can act in generous ways that help and support them.

- Share your knowledge and experience in mentoring relationships.

- Protect your time by being intentional on when and how much you give.

- Model generosity to develop a network of givers that spread it across the organization.

- Ask for permission first, and then offer your help.

Next, we will get to the last building block in humility, which is in relation to the universe, and discuss what transcendence is all about.

four

Humble Leadership in Relation to the Universe

— 10 —

Transcendence

The life of man is of no greater importance
to the universe than that of an oyster.
DAVID HUME

Elevating the World's Consciousness

His goal was to be the first ever trillionaire. He wanted to become "the president of the world." He dreamed of living forever. One of his far-reaching plans was to build work offices on Mars. And he often referred to himself as the greatest real-estate mind in the world.

From his early days, Adam Neumann, the co-founder and former CEO of WeWork, was prone to hyperbole and self-importance. WeWork leased office spaces, renovated them, and re-leased them to artists, entrepreneurs, and small start-ups. But instead of presenting it as the co-working company that it was, Neumann constantly boasted that WeWork was going to change the world. He bragged that "the influence and impact that we're going to have on this earth is going to be big." How exactly did he plan to do that? He was never specific on the details. But due in large part to his personal charisma and powers of persuasion, he convinced wave after wave of investors to put billions of dollars into the company based on outrageous valuations that never materialized.

Neumann combined this "brash self-promotion to the point of self-mythologizing" with eccentric behaviors and blatant nepotism. He bribed employees with company shares to take tequila shots with him at work, he had a special vent installed in his office so he could smoke marijuana, and he often walked around the office barefoot. He hired his wife as the chief brand and impact officer, and gave numerous friends and family members vague and undefined roles and significant privileges at the company.

WeWork's business was faulty at its core: as it gobbled up building after building all over the United States and the world, it was consistently unprofitable due to bad leadership, mismanagement, and over-spending. Neumann didn't see a need for the company to make money. Instead, he pushed for a growth-at-all-costs strategy, with the aim of making WeWork too big to fail. In 2018, he met with Howard Schultz, CEO of Starbucks, who gave him some wise advice. Based on Starbucks' failures when the company grew too fast in a short period of time in the late 2000s, Schultz told Neumann to pause the growth of WeWork for six months in order to fix its efficiency problems. After the meeting with Schultz, when his team asked him if he was planning to listen to the advice, Neumann arrogantly responded with a laugh: "F*** that!" The chaotic growth continued.

In 2019, WeWork was running out of private money, so Neumann reluctantly accepted that he needed to take the company public. However, when the Securities and Exchange Commission examined the company's financial numbers, it became clear that it had lost millions of dollars in its growth frenzy and that its valuation was grossly exaggerated. With the board facing pressure from investors, Neumann was unceremoniously ousted from the company that he founded. WeWork, whose bizarre mission statement was "to elevate the world's consciousness," was forced to lay off hundreds of employees just to keep its doors open.

The universe has a way of humbling self-aggrandizing people like Adam Neumann and reminding them of how small and insignificant they are. While extreme ambition is necessary for success, especially for start-up companies, Neumann's hubris, self-centeredness, and detachment from the realities of the world around him put him on the path to self-destruction. Transcendence, a quality that allows you to realize how insignificant you are as a leader in relation to the larger universe around you, is the final step on your journey as a humbitious leader. A warning, though: things are about to get deep—really deep!

Moral Joy

"I am young and unknown to many of you. I was born and have ever remained in the most humble walks of life. I have no wealthy or popular relations to recommend me. My case is thrown exclusively upon the independent voters of this county, and if elected they will have conferred a favor upon me, for which I shall be unremitting in my labors to compensate. But if the good people in their wisdom shall see fit to keep me in the back ground, I have been too familiar with disappointments to be very much chagrined." You are probably familiar with the words of Abraham Lincoln in his first political announcement in 1832, unpretentiously asking voters to elect him to the Illinois state legislature. What these words reveal is the unique humility of a devoted servant to the public who understands how unimportant he is in the grand scheme of things.

Previous chapters have focused on humble behaviors such as developing self-awareness, gratitude, and open-mindedness. This chapter dives under the surface into the deep-level motivations for humility, such as having a low self-focus and a self-transcendent pursuit, as well as the cognitive core of humility, which consists of wrapping the mind around a transcendent self-concept. The pursuits of humbitious leaders, like Lincoln, are less about their own goals and plans, and more about the larger community and the greater whole, which ultimately causes them to forget the self. When you become aware of something greater than yourself, this self-transcendence protects you from your own excessive ego. If you don't have this transcendence, your humble behaviors may not be sustainable over time or may come across as fake or inauthentic.

As a humbitious transcendent leader, you need to keep your talents and accomplishments, no matter how significant they are, in perspective. You know that you are smart, but you are not all-knowing. You understand that you have personal power, but you are not omnipotent. You see yourself in perspective by realizing that you are just one person in the larger scheme of things. And in that process, you start to realize that you are not the center of your own world. Rather than chasing individual glory, you embrace a collective vision that focuses on the greater good. Most importantly, you realize that you can't reach that vision without the help of others, and that is why you empower them through your appreciation and generosity, as we discussed in previous chapters.

In his outstanding book *The Second Mountain*, cultural commentator David Brooks argues that early on in their lives—when they are climbing their first mountain—most people focus on individual career success and achievements, in a process that is all about building up the ego and defining the self. However, in the second stage of their careers—on their way to the second mountain—the focus needs to shift to a commitment to a larger purpose such as family, community, or philosophy. This transformation involves shedding the ego, connecting with others, and losing the self.

When they reach the peak of their first mountain, people experience happiness that emanates from the various victories for the self. On the second mountain, though, this happiness is slowly replaced with moral joy, a transformational experience where people often get a glimpse into a deeper layer of reality. This type of joy is characterized by a transcendence of the self and a moral elevation; you feel motivated to dedicate your life to connecting with and helping others. Humility, Brooks posits, is a necessary requirement for life on the second mountain. "A narcissist can be happy, but a narcissist can never be joyful, because the surrender of self is the precise thing a narcissist can't do," he explains. In this state of transcendence, you feel more kindness, gratitude, and generosity towards others.

Please note that you don't have to wait till your fifties or sixties to embark on your second mountain and experience this type of moral joy. As a humbitious leader, you can make a commitment to a larger cause earlier on in your career, and as such you can climb both mountains in parallel. You work on your own personal goals and plans while dedicating yourself to a larger cause and recognizing that you are only a small part of the universe. For example, you do everything you can to become an executive or senior partner, but you also aspire to improve employee wellbeing and community benefit. You follow Mahatma Gandhi's advice when he famously said,

"Whatever you do in life will be insignificant, but it is important that you do it, because nobody else will."

Awe and Reverence

The study of transcendence within leadership has taken on a special importance since the concept was introduced as a global imperative at the 2007 World Economic Forum in Davos. Gregory Stebbins, a notable coach and author of *Transcendent Leadership*, is considered one the foremost experts on the topic. He argues that transcendent leaders rise above the *self*, which is focused exclusively on scarcity, and move into the *Self*, which is unbounded and inclusive. (I told you things were going to get deep!) A transcendent leader accepts others' value systems without judgment and displays a reverence that is manifested through an awe for others and a deep reaching to the spirit of being human. This type of leader continuously strives for the highest good for everyone around them.

I recently reached out to Dr. Stebbins to better understand the connections between humility and transcendence. He gracefully explained that while humility is crucial, it has to be used in the right way to lead to true transcendence. "If a leader is being humble and lifts people, then the leader's humility becomes a stepping stone for transcendence. However, if a leader is so humble that nothing shines out, that leader is not going to be able to light up the path for anyone, including self," he articulated. With the right humility that lifts everyone around you, you reside in a graceful state of being. "There is no mental decision of whether to accept something or not. It is hard-wired in the Transcendent Leader," Dr. Stebbins clarified. Similarly, reverence is expanded when you hold humility in your consciousness.

Humility helps you redirect the awe from yourself towards others. You express that awe in the form of, "Oh wow, look what this person is bringing forward for the organization."

What does transcendence look like in everyday leadership behaviors? Dr. Stebbins shared with me the example of a CEO he once coached. This leader was embarking on changing his organization's culture. While the entire executive team was on board with the change, the CFO—a lifelong friend of the CEO—was not. The CEO struggled to accept that the CFO wasn't in alignment with his vision. Transcendence, as we discussed above, is about acceptance. When you are trapped in a state of unawareness about the judgments you have for yourself and those around you, acceptance is hard. It wasn't until Dr. Stebbins helped the CEO dig deep into his own belief system that he finally had an epiphany: he realized that one of the subconscious rules he operated under was to protect the people around him, including the CFO.

With this new insight, the CEO realized that his rule was counterproductive to this situation, and that he couldn't protect the CFO. He also needed to convince himself that just because the CFO was not in alignment, that didn't mean he was a bad guy. As a result, the CEO had an honest conversation with the CFO in which he explained his thinking about the lack of fit. The CFO understood and the CEO helped him find a job with another company that was more aligned with his views of the world. Afterward, Dr. Stebbins told me, the CEO described this experience as one of the most humbling events of his life.

Such states of reverence and awe towards others allow you to see yourself as part of a circle or chain of people. You are dependent on them, and their wellbeing is important to you. This feeling is the perfect antidote to self-centeredness: your main thinking shifts from selfish aspirations towards a concern for your team members' level of engagement with their work, their sense of purpose, their feelings of psychological safety, and their overall happiness. Lin Wang from Sun Yat-sen University in Guangzhou, China, and her colleagues set out to uncover the importance of leader connectedness to others. They studied the level to which leaders were focused on the welfare of others, how deeply committed they were to fulfilling their role relationships, and the extent to which they connected meaningfully with their co-workers and direct reports. Not surprisingly, they found that leaders who displayed this "relational identity" were perceived as more humble by their followers.

As a humbitious transcendent leader, you need to see yourself as part of your team and organization, rather than as the center of it. You value connecting, learning from, and helping people outside of yourself. Your locus of self extends beyond your personal ego to include others. In that sense, humility becomes a "social oil" that enables connections to become smoother and that prevents social jarring. You give away your power and status to elevate and legitimize the development of others. However, as we have discussed on several occasions in this book, this is not about having a low opinion of yourself, but rather about seeing yourself as valuable to others and being willing to sacrifice your personal benefits for the greater good.

Nature and God

The Franklin River is an iconic eighty-mile body of water that flows through the majestic wilderness of southwest Tasmania in Australia. Traveling the river by raft takes about ten days from beginning to end. The trip begins with some easy sections, then makes its way through numerous challenging ravines before it finally opens up on some quiet flat pools and shingle rapids. Marcus Morse, a lecturer at La Trobe University in Australia and an experienced guide and outdoor teacher, wanted to understand the specific experiences that people go through when they embark on such a difficult journey.

Morse asked thirty-two participants who were planning to travel on the Franklin River by raft to report on their experiences through journaling and interviews. The most powerful feeling that the participants described on their return was a sense of humility towards nature. Specifically, they expressed a type of trepidation in being directed towards something that was beyond their imagination in terms of its scale, temporality, and beauty. One person explained: "When you stop and you look around you, you realize how profoundly unimportant you are to the natural flow of life as it unfolds in there. And I think ... that [is a] sort of lesson in humility ... it makes me profoundly aware of how unimportant I am personally, that my species is not the be-all and the end-all." Another traveler noted, "The sense of diminishment that you get which can be both inspiring and also a bit frightening because it's ego dissolving."

What these participants were expressing is a sense of transcendence that people who spend a lot of time in nature sometimes feel: they encounter an awe of nature and a realization of how small and insignificant they are in relation to it. Other people experience similar feelings when they reflect about other larger things, such as God, death, history, or the larger universe. Since the beginning of time, and especially with the emergence of the monolithic religions, most humans have accepted their insignificance in relation to God or some supreme power. It is a form of metaphysical humility in which believers acknowledge their nothingness and the greatness of god who gives them being. They acknowledge their status as a creature, which, without its creator, simply doesn't exist.

Death and Dying

Very closely related to reflecting about a supreme power is reflecting about death. A religious leader I know has a favorite saying: "No matter how much you have, you're going to end up six feet underground, like everyone else!" Ouch. The greatest minds in history, the richest of all kings and queens, and the most powerful of all leaders inevitably succumb to death. The English poet Percy Bysshe Shelley was once traveling through the Egyptian desert when he came across a statue of Ramesses the Great, one of the most powerful pharaohs of his time. Examining the abandoned site, Shelley reflected in a famous sonnet:

> And on the pedestal these words appear:
> My name is Ozymandias, King of Kings;
> Look on my Works, ye Mighty, and despair!
> Nothing beside remains. Round the decay
> Of that colossal Wreck, boundless and bare,
> The lone and level sands stretch far away.

That is one sobering thought for you as a leader. Yes, you may have turned your organization around and achieved great results. Your colleagues and board members have heaped praise on you. Even the business journal has featured a story on you, and your legacy may remain for a few years after you retire. But eventually you are going to leave this life, and the world will still be more or less similar to how it was before you came.

"There is no greater reminder that our time is finite ... than reflecting on our own impending end," warn Brad Stulberg and Steve Magness in *The Passion Paradox*. One of the best ways to gain perspective on our own lack of importance and our place in the world is to make it a habit to periodically think about dying and our own death, regardless of how morbid that sounds. Stulberg and Magness recommend a practice that originated in the Buddhist tradition, where, once a week, you remind yourself of some important truths. For example, on your Friday afternoon commute, you can reflect on the following:

1 You are of the nature to grow old.

2 You are of the nature to have ill health.

3 You are of the nature to die.

4 All that is dear to you is of the nature to change.

5 Your actions are your only true belongings, they are the ground upon which you stand.

While definitely uncomfortable, this practice is a sure way to snap you out of the hustle and bustle of daily life and to help you gain a dose of transcendence and humility.

Whether you reflect on nature, God, death, history, or the ultimate universal truth, you realize how connected everything is and how small and insignificant you are. What are some useful methods for this type of reflection? Neuroscientists at Harvard Medical School have shown that mindfulness meditation, a practice we discussed earlier, can lead to true self-transcendent experiences. These experiences are characterized by the development of positive relationships between the self and others that transcend self-focused needs and increase pro-social characteristics.

Engaging in mindfulness meditation can lead to reflections about compassion, empathy, forgiveness, and love, towards others and towards yourself. To apply this to workplace situations, consider practicing mindfulness meditation before writing an important email or between meetings, with a focus on seeing things objectively and reflecting on how you are a part of a whole. The leadership meditation expert Matthias Birk notes that "taking a few breaths in and out can help lessen your ego's grip." The vital point he makes is that self-transcendence needs to be practiced because it can't be understood by the mind.

Your ego makes you want all the attention and makes you feel like you are constantly the center of the universe. "Ego blocks us from the beauty and history in the world. It stands in the way," notes Ryan Holiday. Only when you accept something greater than yourself can you find your way as a leader. You see yourself accurately and you put your career and achievements in perspective. In the elegant words of leadership expert Bill Treasurer and retired Navy SEAL John Havlik in their book *The Leadership Killer*: "Regardless of how substantial the results you secure, or how high the rank you achieve, or how much wealth you attain, or how many lives you impact, or how much deference or applause you receive, in the grand scheme of things, you ain't sh**!"

How Does a Zipper Work?

With the understanding that you are small and insignificant comes a realization that your knowledge, control, and power are limited. That doesn't mean you give up—it just means that you gain a much-needed humility and groundedness. General Stanley McChrystal understands this better than most leaders. Best known for his role as commander of the Joint Special Operations Command in Iraq and as commander of the International Security Assistance Force in Afghanistan, McChrystal has been described "as the finest warrior and leader of men in combat." I had the pleasure of meeting the general at a dinner party at Trinity University in 2019, after which he made himself available to answer my questions about his leadership style.

As one of the most decorated generals, McChrystal has every reason to believe in his own greatness. But he is very intentional about not falling in that trap. For him, humility in leadership causes you to remind yourself that the attention you get as a leader is not a celebration of you as an individual. The reason people respect you "is not because you are smarter and braver than everyone else," he explained. "You're not personally deserving of the praise and adulation. You remind your ego that it's not about you; the organization will go on without you. It is an inward psychological realization that I'm just a human being."

McChrystal shared that he is not a fan of the passive attitude that can emerge from the idea that there is a greater being who does what He wants and we can't do anything about it. He believes that, as a leader, you have an important role to play, but you should recognize that your role has to be supported by the capabilities of others. McChrystal told me he calls it "a realistic understanding of where you fit and the limits on what you can do."

Humility researchers understand exactly what McChrystal is referring to. In their remarkable research study (that we mentioned earlier in this book), Amy Ou and her co-authors explained that, due to their awareness of their limited knowledge and power, humble leaders understand that they always run the risk of falling short of the standards that they are striving to reach. Let us examine first our limited knowledge, and then we will turn our attention to limited power and control.

Imagine being invited to participate in a study that will test your knowledge of how some common everyday things work. First, you are asked to rate on a scale from 1 to 7 how well you understand how zippers work. Like most people, you will likely give yourself a 6 or 7. After all, you use a zipper several times every day. But then, the researchers ask you to explain, in as much detail as possible, all the steps that are involved in a zipper's operation. Like most participants, you don't have much to say here. You really *don't* know how zippers work. Now, the researchers ask you again to rate on a scale from 1 to 7 how well you understand how zippers work. With your newly acquired humility, you now drop your rating by a few points.

This experiment, conducted by researchers Leonid Rozenblit and Frank Keil from Yale University, demonstrates a phenomenon that we all suffer from as human beings. It is called "the illusion of knowledge": we believe we know much more about things than we actually do. The results are similar when researchers ask people to describe their knowledge of speedometers, piano keys, flush toilets, cylinder locks, helicopters, quartz watches, and sewing machines. It even goes beyond devices and equipment to important issues such as tax policy and foreign relations, GMOs, climate change, and even personal finances. Regardless of the issue being examined, the conclusion is the same: as individual human beings, we know embarrassingly little about the world around us. This appreciation of your limited knowledge should not, however, drive you to despair. Rather, it should give you an appreciation of how vast and complex the universe around you is, and the humility to say, "I don't know, but I will try to find out."

Just as your knowledge is inadequate, your control is also limited. One of the most important Stoic teachings is that some things are under your control and other things are not. Epictetus, the great philosopher, articulated, "The chief task in life is simply this: to identify and separate matters so that I can say clearly to myself which are externals not under my control, and which have to do with the choices I actually control." An important practice is to reflect on what you can control and what you can't. Bad weather that impacts your quarterly sales is not under your control. Other people liking you is not under your control. And no matter how much time you spend being upset about these things, it will not change anything. Instead, you should have the wisdom to admit the futility of your attempts and the humility to focus on what you can control. The things that you can control are your opinions, habits, words, and actions.

Stephen Covey famously captured this notion with his circles of control and concern. If you are not familiar with this concept, imagine two concentric circles: the inner, smaller circle is your circle of control—things that you can influence. The much larger, outer circle is your circle of concern—things that you are constantly worried about and that you complain about, but that you can't influence no matter how hard you try. Covey's advice is similar to Epictetus's: admit that you can't do much about the outer circle, and focus all your attention on the inner circle. Working on your self-awareness, showing gratitude and generosity towards others, and becoming a more humbitious leader all belong in the inner circle.

As a result of your understanding the limits of your control, you accept that your power, especially in large leadership roles with complex responsibilities, is also limited. President Barack Obama eloquently talked about "the irony of the presidential office." He explained that "the longer you're there, the more humble you become, and the more mindful you are that it is beyond your powers individually to move this great country." As a leader, you don't always have the power to influence the results. But what you can do is influence the people who influence the results. Your power consists of creating an environment where humbitiousness is rewarded and where people feel safe expressing their opinions, admitting their mistakes, and unleashing their creativity.

What Next?

Understanding your place in relation to the universe at large is the culmination of your journey towards humbitious leadership. To achieve transcendence, consider developing the following habits:

- Meditate on the vastness of the universe, nature, God, and history.

- Make it a weekly habit to reflect on your own death and on dying.

- Differentiate between what is under your control and what is not.

- Practice mindfulness meditation, in which you reflect on compassion and kindness towards yourself and others.

- Surround yourself with people who will keep you grounded no matter how successful you become.

This is the culmination—and the beginning—of your journey. You are ready. With humility and ambition, nothing can stand in the way between you and high performance!

Acknowledgments

AM DEEPLY GRATEFUL to several individuals for their tremendous help and wise advice.

My amazing team at Page Two Books: Trena White, Jesse Finkelstein, James Harbeck, Meghan O'Neill, Rony Ganon, Lorraine Toor, Peter Cocking, and Melissa Edwards are highly competent in what they do and always available and supportive. They believed in *Humbitious* as much as I did! Neil Pasricha and his great podcast, *Three Books*, is the reason I got introduced to Page Two, and for that I am very grateful to him. Bret Burton, Lizna Makhani, Laura Griffiths, and John Hornbeak reviewed early drafts of the first chapter and offered valuable suggestions. My fellow coaches at MEDI Leadership and fellow speakers at Huron/ Studer Group reviewed early drafts of the first few chapters and provided detailed feedback: Craig Deao, Charles Sorrenson, Jeff Morris, John Fletcher, Mark Noon, Colleen McCrory, Lynne Cunningham, William Barnes, Deb Harrison, Cheryl Foss, Karen Cook, and Wayne Sotile. Several leaders were very gracious and agreed to be interviewed in person, by phone, or by email and to share their expertise and time: Danny Anderson, Deneese "Dee" Jones, Karin Hurt, Joe Folkman, Lee Angus, Janice Kaffer, Stacey Taylor, Brad

Owens, General Stanley McChrystal, Doug Lawson, Daniel Lubetzky, Glenn Robinson, Ryan Holiday, Tasha Eurich, Erol Akdamar, and Gregory Stebbins. Adam Grant agreed to circulate earlier versions of my proposal to potential agents. My chairperson Edward Schumacher and colleagues Jody Rogers, Patrick Shay, Seongwon Choi, Ahreum Han, Sharon Hubenak, Erika Seewald, and Marisela Keppes at the Department of Health Care Administration at Trinity University were very supportive and understanding in terms of the time demands that this project required. My graduate research assistant, Tara Di Pasquale Bradshaw, provided vital research support, while graduate students Nolan Whitely and Grace Mayoral volunteered their time and efforts to help with literature review and referencing. Finally, I am always grateful to the countless blessings of the Almighty God for the accomplishment of this and any other project in my life.

Notes

Introduction

"they are not effective in the long term..." C.W. Ong, R. Roberts, C.A. Arthur, T. Woodman, and S. Akehurst, "The Leader Ship Is Sinking: A Temporal Investigation of Narcissistic Leadership," *Journal of Personality* 84, no. 2 (2016): 237–47.

"humans have always needed to collaborate..." Y.N. Harari, *21 Lessons for the 21st Century* (Spiegel & Grau, 2018).

"as the world is becoming..." B.P. Owens, "Humility in Organizational Leadership" (PhD diss., University of Washington, 2009), proquest.com.

"In the face of this information deluge..." D. Ariely, *Predictably Irrational: The Hidden Forces That Shape Our Decisions* (HarperCollins, 2009).

"And for that..." E.H. Schein and P.A. Schein, *Humble Leadership: The Power of Relationships, Openness, and Trust* (Berrett-Koehler Publishers, 2018).

"some people who know..." Harari, *21 Lessons*, 225.

"a large portion of the population..." "Power Moves: Redefining Leadership by Gender, Generations, and Geographies," EgonZehnder, March 1, 2019, egonzehnder.com/what-we-do/diversity-inclusion/insights/power-moves-redefining-leadership-by-gender-generations-and-geographies.

"the common thread running through..." E.D. Hess and K. Ludwig, *Humility Is the New Smart: Rethinking Human Excellence in the Smart Machine Age* (Berrett-Koehler Publishers, 2017).

Chapter 1: What Is Humble Leadership?

"To help make ends meet..." A. Lester, "New Zealand's Prime Minister, Jacinda Ardern, Is Young, Forward-Looking, and Unabashedly Liberal—Call Her the Anti-Trump," *Vogue*, February 14, 2018, vogue.com/article/jacinda-ardern-new-zealand-prime-minister-vogue-march-2018-issue.

"she noticed that some girls..." M. Dowd, "Lady of the Rings: Jacinda Rules," *New York Times*, September 8, 2018, nytimes.com/2018/09/08/opinion/sunday/jacinda-ardern-new-zealand-prime-minister.html.

"She called Waring..." L. Fitzpatrick and C. Quackenbush, "Jacinda Ardern, New Zealand's 37-Year-Old Leader, Rolls up Her Sleeves," *Time*, November 20, 2017, time.com/5028891/jacinda-ardern-worlds-youngest-female-leader-new-zealand.

"The faculty described her..." Fitzpatrick and Quackenbush, "Jacinda Ardern."

"the same modest three-bedroom..." Fitzpatrick and Quackenbush, "Jacinda Ardern."

"'Many people, myself included...'" A.N. Bissett, "'Jacinda Is a Beacon of Hope': How New Zealand's Prime Minister Has Helped Heal a Heart-broken Nation," *Independent*, March 23, 2019, independent.co.uk/news/world/australasia/jacinda-ardern-new-zealand-shootings-attack-christchurch-mosque-a8835561.html.

"In all, he killed..." A. Lester, "The Roots of Jacinda Ardern's Extraordinary Leadership After Christchurch," *New Yorker*, March 23, 2019, newyorker.com/culture/culture-desk/what-jacinda-arderns-leadership-means-to-new-zealand-and-to-the-world.

"And nothing could have..." I. Tharoor, "The Racist Theory That Underlies Terrorism in New Zealand and the Trump Presidency," *Washington Post*, March 18, 2019, washingtonpost.com/world/2019/03/18/racist-theory-that-links-terror-new-zealand-trump-presidency.

"'We are forever grateful...'" Lester, "Roots."

"The most-shared image..." T. MacDonald, "5 Lessons That Justin Trudeau Can Learn from Jacinda Ardern, Celebrated Prime Minister of New Zealand," *MTL Blog*, March 27, 2019, mtlblog.com/opinions/5-lessons-that-justin-trudeau-can-learn-from-jacinda-ardern-celebrated-prime-minister-of-new-zealand.

"'You may have chosen us...'" S. Mahtani and A. Fifield, "'You Will Never Hear Me Mention His Name': New Zealand's Ardern Vows to Deny Accused Shooter Notoriety," *Washington Post*, March 19, 2019, washingtonpost.com/world/asia_pacific/you-will-never-hear-me-mention-his-name-

new-zealands-ardern-hopes-to-deny-shooter-notoriety/2019/03/19/
b4d163b8-49b5-11e9-8cfc-2c5d0999c21e_story.html.

"For the citizens of New Zealand..." S. Goulopoulos, "How Jacinda Ardern
Handled Her First Terrorism Situation Shows Her Strength and
Humility," *Whimn*, March 16, 2019. (Unfortunately, the website and
story have since been removed.)

"So far, it seems that Ardern..." Bissett, "Beacon of Hope."

"'One of the criticisms...'" Dowd, "Lady of the Rings."

"originates from the Latin..." J.A. Morris, C.M. Brotheridge, and J.C. Urbanski,
"Bringing Humility to Leadership: Antecedents and Consequences of
Leader Humility," *Human Relations* 58, no. 1 (2005): 1323–50.

"viewed humility as desirable..." R. Holiday, "Humility Kills Pride," Daily Stoic,
dailystoic.com/humility-kills-pride.

"Seneca, the pioneering..." D. Robertson, *How to Think Like a Roman Emperor:
The Stoic Philosophy of Marcus Aurelius* (St. Martin's Press, 2019).

"the path to enlightenment..." P. Mishra, *An End to Suffering: The Buddha in the
World* (Farrar, Straus, and Giroux, 2004).

"the Taoists conceived..." Lao-tzu and S. Mitchell, *Tao Te Ching: A New English
Version* (HarperCollins, 2006).

"described the humble person..." Q. Kong, *The Analects of Confucius*, translated
by S. Leys (W.W. Norton & Company, 1997).

"without humility, the mind..." B. Spinoza and E.M. Curley, *A Spinoza Reader:
The Ethics and Other Works* (Princeton University Press, 1994).

"Immanuel Kant stressed that..." J. Grenberg, *Kant and the Ethics of Humility:
A Story of Dependence, Corruption, and Virtue* (Cambridge University
Press, 2005), 133.

"who reasoned that humility..." A. Comte-Sponville, *A Small Treatise on the
Great Virtues* (Henry Holt & Company, 2001).

"A recent refocus on humility..." C. Peterson and M. Seligman, *Character
Strengths and Virtues: A Handbook and Classification* (Oxford University
Press, 2004).

"to be humble is not..." J. Tangney, "Humility: Theoretical Perspectives,
Empirical Findings, and Directions for Future Research," *Journal of
Social and Clinical Psychology* 19, no. 1 (2000): 71–72.

"you are engaging in..." A. Havard, *Created for Greatness: The Power of
Magnanimity* (Scepter, 2014).

"you can be open to new ideas..." Morris, Botheridge, and Urbanski, "Bringing Humility."

"When a leader is able..." K.E. Weick, "Leadership as the Legitimization of Doubt," in W. Bennis, G.M. Spreitzer, and T.G. Cummings (eds.), *The Future of Leadership: Today's Top Leadership Thinkers Speak to Tomorrow's Leaders* (Jossey-Bass, 2001), 110.

"describes this quality as..." Owens, "Humility in Organizational."

"you aren't just aware that..." Tangney, "Humility: Theoretical Perspectives."

"often referred to as..." Havard, *Created for Greatness.*

"When we lack connection..." R. Holiday, *Ego Is the Enemy* (Portfolio, Penguin, 2016), 139–40.

"Harper is credited for many..." A. Kaissi, *Intangibles: The Unexpected Traits of High Performing Healthcare Leaders* (Health Administration Press, 2017).

"When you leave Extreme Blue..." B. Taylor, "On the 'Battle for Talent' and the Power of 'Humbition,'" *Harvard Business Review*, February 27, 2008, hbr.org/2008/02/on-the-battle-for-talent-and-t.

"We were surprised..." J.C. Collins, *Good to Great: Why Some Companies Make the Leap—And Others Don't* (Harper Business, 2001), 12.

"They demonstrate professional will..." J.C. Collins, "Level-5 Leadership: The Triumph of Humility and Fierce Resolve," *Harvard Business Review* 79, no. 1 (2000): 1–12.

"teams experimented freely with..." B.P. Owens, "Leader Trait Couplings: The Synergy of Humility & Competence, the Paradox of Humility & Narcissism," *Academy of Management Proceedings* 2012, no. 1: 16319, doi. org/10.5465/AMBPP.2012.16319abstract.

"A study of Portuguese managers..." M. Sousa and D. van Dierendonck, "Servant Leadership and the Effect of the Interaction Between Humility, Action, and Hierarchical Power on Follower Engagement," *Journal of Business Ethics* 141, no. 1 (2017): 13–25, doi.org/10.1007/s10551-015-2725-y.

"this approach can only have an impact..." R.K. Greenleaf and L.C. Spears, *Servant Leadership: A Journey into the Nature of Legitimate Power and Greatness* (Paulist Press, 2002).

"The great Greek philosopher reasoned..." Havard, *Created for Greatness.*

"a twofold virtue is necessary..." T. Aquinas, *Summa Theologica* II-II, q.162, a.1c; cf.

"confidence, without humility..." K. Hurt, "Humility Matters: 9 Ways Confident Leaders Remain Humble," *Let's Grow Leaders*, September 4, 2012, letsgrowleaders.com/2012/09/04/humility.

"while sometimes people think..." K. Hurt, email exchange with author, 2019.

"You lead for the long run..." R. Hougaard and J. Carter, *The Mind of the Leader: How to Lead Yourself, Your People, and Your Organization for Extraordinary Results* (Harvard Business Review Press, 2018).

"'humble, hungry, and smart...'" E. Akdamar, interview with author, 2018.

"in his insightful book..." P. Lencioni, *The Ideal Team Player: How to Recognize and Cultivate the Three Essential Virtues: A Leadership Fable* (John Wiley and Sons, 2016).

"the hunger and smarts are not..." Lencioni, *Ideal Team Player*, 44.

"For those of us climbing..." Lencioni, 45.

"Humility can actually be..." B. Taylor, "If Humility Is So Important, Why Are Leaders So Arrogant?" *Harvard Business Review*, October 15, 2018, hbr.org/2018/10/if-humility-is-so-important-why-are-leaders-so-arrogant.

"He threw frequent tantrums..." R.E. Riggio, "Why Steve Jobs Is a Leadership Nightmare," *Psychology Today*, February 7, 2012, psychologytoday.com/ca/blog/cutting-edge-leadership/201202/why-steve-jobs-is-leadership-nightmare.

"some psychologists even suggesting..." G. Henriques, "Was Steve Jobs' Narcissism Justified?" *Psychology Today,* January 20, 2012, psychologytoday.com/us/blog/theory-knowledge/201201/was-steve-jobs-narcissism-justified.

"I didn't see it then..." S. Jobs, "You've Got to Find What You Love," *Stanford News*, June 14, 2005, news.stanford.edu/2005/06/14/jobs-061505.

"it was exactly this unusual combination..." B.P. Owens, A.S. Wallace, and D.A. Waldman, "Leader Narcissism and Follower Outcomes: The Counterbalancing Effect of Leader Humility," *Journal of Applied Psychology* 100, no. 4 (2015): 1203-13, doi.org/10.1037/a0038698.

"when leader humility was high..." Owens, Wallace, and Waldman, "Leader Narcissism."

"narcissism and humility can coexist..." H. Zhang, A.Y. Ou, A.S. Tsui, and H. Wang, "CEO Humility, Narcissism, and Firm Innovation: A Paradox Perspective on CEO Traits," *The Leadership Quarterly* 28, no. 5 (2017): 585-604, doi.org/10.1016/j.leaqua.2017.01.003.

"Narcissism gives you..." A. Grant, "Tapping into the Power of Humble Narcissism," TED Ideas, March 14, 2018, ideas.ted.com/tapping-into-the-power-of-humble-narcissism.

Chapter 2: The Benefits of Humble Leadership

"We love our tea..." A. Svokos, "Alex Morgan's Tea Cup World Cup Goal Pose Causes Brits to Freak Out," ABC News, July 3, 2019, abcnews.go.com/Sports/alex-morgans-tea-cup-world-cup-goal-pose/story?id=64111142.

"All of that stardom…" M. Fornoff, "Double Standard? Players, Fans Push Back on Criticism of U.S. Women's Soccer," MPR News, July 8, 2019, mprnews.org/story/2019/07/07/players-fans-push-back-criticism-us-womens-soccer.

"calling them smug and entitled…" E. Sweeney, "Arrogant, Entitled, and Self-Centred, the US Women's Soccer Team Couldn't Be More Trumpian," *Independent.ie,* July 7, 2019, independent.ie/sport/soccer/womens-world-cup/eamonn-sweeney-arrogant-entitled-and-self-centred-the-us-womens-soccer-team-couldnt-be-more-trumpian-38289699.html.

"We have the best…" J. Prince-Wright, "USWNT: 'We Have Best Team and Second Best Team in World,'" NBC Sports, June 17, 2019, soccer.nbc sports.com/2019/06/17/uswnt-we-have-best-team-and-second-best-team-in-world/.

"they did the opposite…" A. Thomas, "The USWNT Is Exactly as Arrogant as You Perceive It to Be," *SB Nation,* July 3, 2019, sbnation.com/soccer/2019/7/3/20680668/arrogance-england-united-states-world-cup.

"It's important that our team…" Thomas, "The USWNT."

"We have the utmost…" R. Bachman, "U.S. Soccer Star Megan Rapinoe Responds to Critics, Saying She's 'Deeply American,'" *Wall Street Journal,* July 3, 2019, wsj.com/articles/u-s-soccer-star-megan-rapinoe-responds-to-critics-saying-shes-deeply-american-11562175592.

"the truly humble tended to rate…" Tangney, "Humility: Theoretical Perspectives."

"the truly humble never know…" K. Singh, "Humility and Simplicity 1967," *KirpalSingh-Teachings.org.* kirpalsingh-teachings.org/index.php/sv/circular-letters/562-humility-and-simplicity.html.

"humility may be 'simply…'" Tangney, "Humility: Theoretical Perspectives," 78.

"the one developed by Brad Owens…" B.P. Owens, M.D. Johnson, and T.R. Mitchell, "Expressed Humility in Organizations: Implications for Performance, Teams, and Leadership," *Organization Science* 24, no. 5 (2013): 1517–38, dx.doi.org/10.1287/orsc.1120.0795.

"They invited 144 students…" Owens, Johnson, and Mitchell, "Expressed Humility."

"humble students were more satisfied…" W.C. Rowatt, C. Powers, V. Targhetta, J. Comer, S. Kennedy, and J. LaBouff, "Development and Initial Validation of an Implicit Measure of Humility Relative to Arrogance," *Journal of Positive Psychology* 1, no. 4 (2006): 198–211, doi.org/10.1080/17439760600885671.

"found strong connections between different…" A. Zawadzka and J. Zalewska, "Can Humility Bring Happiness in Life? The Relationship Between Life Aspirations, Subjective Well-Being, and Humility," *Roczniki Psychologiczne* 16, no. 3 (2013): 433–49.

"Walker set out to identify…" S. Walker, *The Captain Class: The Hidden Force That Creates the World's Greatest Teams* (Random House, 2017).

"she is modeling how to grow…" B.P. Owens and D.R. Hekman, "How Does Leader Humility Influence Team Performance? Exploring the Mechanisms of Contagion and Collective Promotion Focus," *Academy of Management Journal* 59, no. 3 (2016): 1088–1111, doi.org/10.5465/amj.2013.0660.

"as a result, the team displays…" Owens, "Leader Trait Couplings."

"Team members feel efficacious…" A. Rego, B. Owens, S. Leal, A.I. Melo, M.P. Cunha, L. Gonçalves, and P. Ribeiro, "How Leader Humility Helps Teams to Be Humbler, Psychologically Stronger, and More Effective: A Moderated Mediation Model," *The Leadership Quarterly* 28, no. 5 (2017): 639–58, doi.org/10.1016/j.leaqua.2017.02.002.

"the team is better equipped…" A. Rego, B. Owens, K.C. Yam, D. Bluhm, M.P. Cunha, A. Silard, and W. Liu, "Leader Humility and Team Performance: Exploring the Mediating Mechanisms of Team PsyCap and Task Allocation Effectiveness," *Journal of Management* 45, no. 3 (2019): 1009–33, doi.org/10.1177/0149206316688941.

"They were all part of the 'Marshmallow Challenge…'" T. Wujec, "Build a Tower, Build a Team," TED YouTube channel, April 22, 2010, youtube.com/watch?v=HO_yKBitO8M.

"introducing the concept of psychological safety…" A.C. Edmondson, *The Fearless Organization: Creating Psychological Safety in the Workplace for Learning, Innovation, and Growth* (John Wiley & Sons, 2019).

"while she had been conducting…" A.C. Edmondson, keynote "The Fearless Organization: Creating Psychological Safety in the Workplace for Compassion and Collaboration," Compassion in Action Healthcare Conference, The Schwartz Center for Compassionate Healthcare, Boston, September 9, 2019.

"greater involvement of unit employees…" I.M. Nembhard and A.C. Edmondson, "Making It Safe: The Effects of Leader Inclusiveness and Professional Status on Psychological Safety and Improvement Efforts in Health Care Teams," *Journal of Organizational Behavior* 27, no. 7 (2006): 941–66, doi.org/10.1002/job.413.

"they could be themselves without fear..." K.N. Walters and D.L. Diab, "Humble Leadership: Implications for Psychological Safety and Follower Engagement," *Journal of Leadership Studies* 10, no. 2 (2016): 7–18, doi.org/10. 1002/jls.21434.

"These conditions unleash..." Y. Wang, J. Liu, and Y. Zhu, "Humble Leadership, Psychological Safety, Knowledge Sharing, and Follower Creativity: A Cross-Level Investigation," *Frontiers in Psychology* 9 (2018): 1727, doi. org/10.3389/fpsyg.2018.01727.

"The best bosses are..." S. Shellenbarger, "The Best Bosses Are Humble Bosses," *Wall Street Journal*, October 9, 2018, wsj.com/articles/the-best-bosses-are-humble-bosses-1539092123.

"'My guess is that...'" B. Owens, email exchange with author, 2019.

"While leaders claim..." J. Harter, "Employee Engagement on the Rise in the U.S. Economy," Gallup, August 26, 2018, news.gallup.com/poll/241649/employee-engagement-rise.aspx.

"play a major role in improving..." D.M. Cable, *Alive at Work: The Neuroscience of Helping Your People Love What They Do* (Harvard Business Review Press, 2018).

"If I admit lack of knowledge..." Cable, *Alive at Work*, 125.

"the path by which humble leadership..." B.P. Owens and D.R. Hekman, "Modeling How to Grow: An Inductive Examination of Humble Leader Behaviors, Contingencies, and Outcomes," *Academy of Management Journal* 55, no. 4 (2012): 787–818, doi.org/10.5465/amj.2010.0441.

"conducted 360-degree feedback assessments..." J. Zenger and J. Folkman, "We Like Leaders Who Underrate Themselves," *Harvard Business Review*, November 10, 2015, hbr.org/2015/11/we-like-leaders-who-underrate-themselves.

"'a humble leader always assumes...'" J. Folkman, email exchange with author, 2019.

"middle managers led by humble CEOs..." A.Y. Ou, A.S. Tsui, A.J. Kinicki, D.A. Waldman, Z. Xiao, and L.J. Song, "Humble Chief Executive Officers' Connections to Top Management Team Integration and Middle Managers' Responses," *Administrative Science Quarterly* 59, no. 1 (2014): 34–72, doi.org/10.1177/0001839213520131.

"you need to psychologically empower..." Y. Chen, B. Liu, L. Zhang, and S. Qian, "Can Leader 'Humility' Spark Employee 'Proactivity'? The Mediating Role of Psychological Empowerment," *Leadership & Organization Development Journal* 39, no. 3 (2018): 326–39, doi.org/10.1108/LODJ-10-2017-0307.

"interviewed German organizational leaders…" S. Strüfing, "Humble Leadership: Relevance to Employees' Creativity and Innovation Under the Consideration of Time Pressure" (master's thesis, University of Twente, 2014).

"They displayed more creativity…" J. Wang, Z. Zhang, and M. Jia, "Understanding How Leader Humility Enhances Employee Creativity: The Roles of Perspective Taking and Cognitive Reappraisal," *Journal of Applied Behavioral Science* 53, no. 1 (2017): 5-31, doi.org/10.1177/0021886316678907.

"employees who interact with you will display…" F. Zhou and Y.J. Wu, "How Humble Leadership Fosters Employee Innovation Behavior: A Two-Way Perspective on the Leader-Employee Interaction," *Leadership & Organization Development Journal* 39, no. 3 (2018): 377, doi.org/10.1108/LODJ-07-2017-0181.

"trust that you will be fair and impartial…" C. Liu, "Does Humble Leadership Behavior Promote Employees' Voice Behavior? A Dual Mediating Model," *Open Journal of Business and Management* 4 (2016): 731-40, dx.doi.org/10.4236/ojbm.2016.44071.

"they are more likely to speak up…" X. Lin, Z.X. Chen, H.H.M. Tse, W. Wei, and C. Ma, "Why and When Employees Like to Speak up More Under Humble Leaders? The Roles of Personal Sense of Power and Power Distance," *Journal of Business Ethics* 158, no. 4 (2019): 937-50, doi.org/10.1007/s10551-017-3704-2.

"The CEO was always complaining…" L. Angus, interview with author, 2019.

"More than education…" D.L. Coutu, "How Resilience Works," *Harvard Business Review* (May 2002), hbr.org/2002/05/how-resilience-works.

"view setbacks as temporary…" M.E.P. Seligman, "Building Resilience," *Harvard Business Review* (April 2011), hbr.org/2011/04/building-resilience.

"were more likely to display…" Rego et al., "Leader Humility and Team."

"more likely to perform well on their work-related…" Ou et al., "Humble Chief Executive."

"enables the organization to become more fluid…" A.Y. Ou, D.A. Waldman, and S.J. Peterson, "Do Humble CEOs Matter? An Examination of CEO Humility and Firm Outcomes," *Journal of Management* 44, no. 3 (2018): 1147-73, doi.org/10.1177/0149206315604187.

"significantly higher return on assets…" Ou, Waldman, and Peterson, "CEOs Matter."

"to have a realistic view of themselves…" D. Vera and A. Rodriguez-Lopez, "Strategic Virtues: Humility as a Source of Competitive Advantage,"

Organizational Dynamics 33, no. 4 (2004): 393-408, doi.org/10.1016/j.
orgdyn.2004.09.006.

Chapter 3: Determinants and Moderators of Humble Leadership

"Stacey Taylor was very excited..." S. Taylor, interview with author, 2019.
"'You go to a class...'" C.S. Dweck, *Mindset: The New Psychology of Success*
(Ballantine Books, 2008), 8.
"a study of eighty-five teams in China..." L. Wang, B.P. Owens, J.J. Li, and L. Shi,
"Exploring the Affective Impact, Boundary Conditions, and Antecedents
of Leader Humility," *Journal of Applied Psychology* 103, no. 9 (2018):
1019-38, doi.org/10.1037/apl0000314.
"Basing his ideas on thirty interviews..." Owens, "Humility in Organizational," 9..
"connection between self-esteem and humility..." J. Folkman, "Do You Know
Yourself? You're Not as Good or Bad of a Leader as You Think," *Forbes*,
December 30, 2019, forbes.com/sites/joefolkman/2020/12/30/do-you-
know-yourself-youre-not-as-good-or-bad-of-a-leader-as-you-think.
"leaders with relational identity..." Wang et al., "Affective Impact."
"religious individuals viewed humility..." Folkman, "Do You Know."
"'My faith plays...'" D. Jones, interview with author, 2019.
"extreme emphasis on performance..." Folkman, "Do You Know," 69.
"'I never stopped becoming...'" Collins, *Good to Great*, 20.
"'I left one of my last...'" Owens, "Humility in Organizational," 62.
"I actually had a really..." Owens and Hekman, "Modeling," 795.
"why decisive, take-charge types..." P. Addison, "Why Churchill Lost in 1945,"
BBC History, February 17, 2011, bbc.co.uk/history/worldwars/wwtwo/
election_01.shtml.
"'Yes. We had a conflict...'" J. Kaffer, interview with author, 2019.
"'It becomes really problematic...'" Jones, interview with author, 2019.
"members of seventy-two teams..." J.J. Hu, B. Erdogan, K. Jiang, T.N. Bauer,
and S. Liu, "Leader Humility and Team Creativity: The Role of Team
Information Sharing, Psychological Safety, and Power Distance,"
Journal of Applied Psychology 103, no. 3 (2018): 313-23, doi.org/10.1037/
apl0000277.
"not everyone wants..." J.J. Hu, B. Erdogan, K. Jiang, and T.N. Bauer,
"Research: When Being a Humble Leader Backfires," *Harvard Business
Review*, April 4, 2018, hbr.org/2018/04/research-when-being-a-
humble-leader-backfires.

"'But then, some of them…'" D. Anderson, interview with author, 2019.

"when employee humility was lower…" X. Qin, X. Liu, J.A. Brown, X. Zheng, and B.P. Owens, "Humility Harmonized? Exploring Whether and How Leader and Employee Humility (In)Congruence Influences Employee Citizenship and Deviance Behaviors," *Journal of Business Ethics* 170 (2019): 147–65, doi.org/10.1007/s10551-019-04250-4.

"'although expressing humility could…'" J. Mao, C. Chiu, B.P. Owens, J.A. Brown, and J. Liao, "Growing Followers: Exploring the Effects of Leader Humility on Follower Self-Expansion, Self-Efficacy, and Performance," *Journal of Management Studies* 56, no. 2 (2019): 343–71, doi.org/10.1111/joms.12395.

Chapter 4: Self-Awareness

"'Nuh-uh, I don't believe it…'" M. Isaac, "'I'm a Terrible Person': Behind the Epic Meltdown that Ended Travis Kalanick," *Vanity Fair*, September 3, 2019, vanityfair.com/news/2019/08/behind-the-epic-meltdown-that-ended-travis-kalanick.

"Travis Kalanick and a couple…" R. Shah, "Uber CEO Kalanick Argues with Driver over Falling Fares," Bloomberg Quicktake, February 28, 2017, YouTube video, 6:11, youtube.com/watch?v=gTEDYckNqns.

"'I'm a terrible person…'" M. Isaac, *Super Pumped: The Battle for Uber* (W.W. Norton, 2019).

"rarely listened to others…" M. Isaac, "Inside Uber's Aggressive, Unrestrained Workplace Culture," *New York Times*, February 22, 2017, nytimes.com/2017/02/22/technology/uber-workplace-culture.html.

"Like so many rock-star entrepreneurs…" T. Eurich, "The Biggest Mistake That CEOs Like Uber's Travis Kalanick Make," *CNBC*, June 12, 2017, cnbc.com/2017/06/12/the-biggest-mistake-that-ceos-like-ubers-travis-kalanick-make-commentary.html.

"'self-awareness is the will…'" T. Eurich, *Insight: Why We're Not as Self-Aware as We Think, and How Seeing Ourselves Clearly Helps Us Succeed at Work and in Life* (Currency, 2017), 24.

"on a good day, most of us…" T. Eurich, "Increase Your Self-Awareness with One Simple Fix," TEDxMileHigh, November 2017, TED video, 17:17, ted.com/talks/tasha_eurich_increase_your_self_awareness_with_one_simple_fix.

"Follow effective action…" J. Porter, "Why You Should Make Time for Self-Reflection (Even If You Hate Doing It)," *Harvard Business Review*,

March 21, 2017, hbr.org/2017/03/why-you-should-make-time-for-self-reflection-even-if-you-hate-doing-it.

"An 'introspector...'" T. Eurich, "What Self-Awareness Really Is (and How to Cultivate It)," *Harvard Business Review*, January 4, 2018, hbr.org/2018/01/what-self-awareness-really-is-and-how-to-cultivate-it.

"make better decisions..." D.S. Ridley, P.A Schutz, R.S. Glanz, and C.E. Weinstein, "Self-Regulated Learning: The Interactive Influence of Metacognitive Awareness and Goal-Setting," *Journal of Experimental Education* 60, no. 4 (1992): 293-306, doi.org/10.1080/00220973. 1992.9943867.

"have better relations with others..." C. Fletcher and C. Bailey, "Assessing Self-Awareness: Some Issues and Methods," *Journal of Managerial Psychology* 18, no. 5 (2003): 395-404, doi.org/10.1108/02683940310484008.

"have higher self-esteem..." P.J. Silvia and M.E. O'Brien, "Self-Awareness and Constructive Functioning: Revisiting 'the Human Dilemma,'" *Journal of Social and Clinical Psychology* 23, no. 4 (2004): 475-89, doi.org/10.1521/jscp.23.4.475.40307.

"typically report healthier wellbeing..." A. Sutton, H.M. Williams, and C.W. Allinson, "A Longitudinal, Mixed Method Evaluation of Self-Awareness Training in the Workplace," *European Journal of Training and Development* 39, no. 7 (2015): 610-27, doi.org/10.1108/EJTD-04-2015-0031.

"those who were more successful..." M. Higgs and D. Rowland, "Emperors with Clothes On: The Role of Self-Awareness in Developing Effective Change Leadership," *Journal of Change Management* 10, no. 4 (2010): 369-85, doi.org/10.1080/14697017.2010.516483.

"self-aware leaders were one-sixth..." J. Roper, "Are Your High-Potential Leaders at Risk of Derailment?" *HR Magazine*, October 7, 2015, hrmagazine.co.uk/article-details/are-your-high-potential-leaders-at-risk-of-derailment.

"strong relationships between leader self-awareness..." A.G. Tekleab, H.P. Sims, S. Yun, P.E. Tesluk, and J. Cox, "Are We on the Same Page? Effects of Self-Awareness of Empowering and Transformational Leadership," *Journal of Leadership & Organizational Studies* 14, no. 3 (2008): 185-201, doi.org/10.1177/1071791907311069.

"own performance and effectiveness..." J.J. Sosik, "Self-Other Agreement on Charismatic Leadership: Relationships with Work Attitudes and Managerial Performance," *Group & Organization Management* 26, no. 4 (2001): 484-511, doi.org/10.1177/1059601101264005.

"their organizations' outcomes..." O. Atuma and M.E. Agwu, "Self-Awareness and Organizational Performance in the Nigerian Banking Sector," *European Journal of Research and Reflection in Management Sciences* 3, no. 1 (2018): 53-70, idpublications.org/wp-content/uploads/2014/12/Self-Awareness-and-Organizational-performance-Full-Paper.pdf.

"'Because it means appreciating...'" Eurich, *Insight*, 90.

"tend to see the self as a cause..." Silvia and O'Brien, "Self-Awareness and Constructive."

"enables true confidence..." Sutton, Williams, and Allinson, "Longitudinal."

"they tend to rate themselves..." J.W. Fleenor, C.D. McCauley, and S. Brutus, "Self-Other Rating Agreement and Leader Effectiveness," *Leadership Quarterly* 7, no. 4 (1996): 487-506, doi.org/10.1016/S1048-9843(96) 90003-X.

"tried to serve an organizational purpose..." Higgs and Rowland, "Emperors."

"Informers tend to have..." M. Naaman, J. Boase, and C.-H. Lai, "Is It Really About Me?: Message Content in Social Awareness Streams," *Proceedings of the 2010 ACM Conference on Computer Supported Cooperative Work* (2010): 189-92, doi.org/10.1145/1718918.1718953.

"'Humble leaders are Informers...'" T. Eurich, email exchange with author, 2020.

"research has shown that blind spots..." S. Vazire and E.N. Carlson, "Others Sometimes Know Us Better Than We Know Ourselves," *Current Directions in Psychological Science* 20, no. 2 (2011): 104-8, doi.org/10. 1177/0963721411402478.

"examined these types of blind spots..." Vazire and Carlson, "Others Sometimes."

"leaders who receive unfavorable..." J.W. Smither, M. London, and R.R. Reilly, "Does Performance Improve Following Multisource Feedback? A Theoretical Model, Meta-Analysis, and Review of Empirical Findings," *Personnel Psychology* 58, no. 1 (2005): 33-66, doi.org/10.1111/j.1744-6570.2005.514_1.x.

"To get the other 75 percent..." J. Porter, "6 Steps Leaders Can Take to Get the Most Out of Feedback," *Harvard Business Review*, September 10, 2019, hbr.org/2019/09/6-steps-leaders-can-take-to-get-the-most-out-of-feedback.

"'prediction-other' rating was a better explainer...'" S.N. Taylor, M. Wang, and Y. Zhan, "Going Beyond Self-Other Rating Comparison to Measure Leader Self-Awareness," *Journal of Leadership Studies* 6, no. 2 (2012): 6-31, doi.org/10.1002/jls.21235.

"If you don't know…" P. McCord, *Powerful: Building a Culture of Freedom and Responsibility* (Silicon Guild, 2017), 47.

"are also in the top percentile…" J. Folkman, "Top Ranked Leaders Know This Secret: Ask for Feedback," *Forbes*, January 8, 2015, forbes.com/sites/joefolkman/2015/01/08/top-ranked-leaders-know-this-secret-ask-for-feedback.

"leaders who believe they have a fixed ability…" Folkman, email exchange with author, 2019.

"they are more likely to take the time…" Folkman, "Top Ranked."

"identify a small group of people…" Eurich, "Really Is."

"you can approach a trusted colleague…" E. Hoekstra, A. Bell, and S.R. Peterson, "Humility in Leadership: Abandoning the Pursuit of Unattainable Perfection," *Executive Ethics: Ethical Dilemmas and Challenges for the C-Suite* (Information Age Publishing, 2008).

"seek specific recommendations…" J. Porter, "How Leaders Can Get Honest, Productive Feedback," *Harvard Business Review*, January 8, 2019, hbr.org/2019/01/how-leaders-can-get-honest-productive-feedback.

"make a plan to take action…" Porter, "Productive Feedback."

"Feedback is screechy…" Z. Friedman, "*New York Times* Bestselling Author Kim Scott on the Art of Feedback," *Forbes*, July 24, 2018, forbes.com/sites/zackfriedman/2018/07/24/kim-scott-feedback-radical-candor.

"is more future-oriented…" J. Yoon, H. Blunden, A. Kristal, and A. Whillans, "Why Asking for Advice Is More Effective than Asking for Feedback," *Harvard Business Review*, September 20, 2019, hbr.org/2019/09/why-asking-for-advice-is-more-effective-than-asking-for-feedback.

"If feedback is past tense…" M. Goldsmith and M. Reiter, *What Got You Here Won't Get You There: How Successful People Become Even More Successful!* (Profile Books, 2012), 173.

"I want to be a better listener…" Goldsmith and Reiter, *What Got You Here*, 171.

"It is paying attention…" Hougaard and Carter, *Mind of the Leader*.

"You are not your thoughts…" C. Wakeman, *No Ego: How Leaders Can Cut the Cost of Workplace Drama, End Entitlement, and Drive Big Results* (St. Martin's Press, 2017).

"this separation allows you to build…" B. Stulberg and S. Magness, *The Passion Paradox: A Guide to Going All In, Finding Success, and Discovering the Benefits of an Unbalanced Life* (Rodale Books, 2019).

"By taking yourself out of the picture…" Stulberg and Magness, *Passion Paradox*.

"When you cultivate mindfulness…" J. Kabat-Zinn, *Wherever You Go, There You Are: Mindfulness Meditation in Everyday Life* (Hachette, 2005).

"My ego had run amok..." R. Hougaard, J. Carter, and M. Afton, "Self-Awareness Can Help Leaders More than an MBA Can," *Harvard Business Review,* January 12, 2018, hbr.org/2018/01/self-awareness-can-help-leaders-more-than-an-mba-can.

Chapter 5: Self-Reflection

"these very attributes may result..." Hoekstra, Bell, and Peterson, "Abandoning."

"it gets filtered and flavored..." Hoekstra, Bell, and Peterson, "Abandoning."

"are essential for the development of humility..." Hoekstra, Bell, and Peterson, "Abandoning."

"identifying twelve virtues..." B. Franklin, *The Autobiography of Benjamin Franklin* [1791] (Createspace, 2019).

"creating a log book and making a black mark..." D.J. Bobb, *Humility: An Unlikely Biography of America's Greatest Virtue* (Thomas Nelson Books, 2013).

"study examining the daily calendars..." M.E. Porter, N. Nohria, T. Gentile, D. McGinn, and S. Higgins, "Spotlight: The Leader's Calendar," *Harvard Business Review* (July–August 2018), 19, hbr.org/2018/07/the-leaders-calendar.

"A crowded world thinks..." E. Moore, "Chronicle Interview from 1996: The Thoughtful Words of John Graves," *Houston Chronicle,* July 31, 2013, houstonchronicle.com/entertainment/article/Chronicle-interview-from-1996-The-thoughtful-4698380.php.

"participants were placed in empty rooms..." T.D. Wilson, D.A. Reinhard, E.C. Westgate, D.T. Gilbert, N. Ellerbeck, C. Hahn, C.L. Brown, and A. Shaked, "Just Think: The Challenges of the Disengaged Mind," *Science* 345, no. 6192 (2014): 75–77, doi.org/10.1126/science.1250830.

"It is difficult to understand yourself..." R. Holiday, *Stillness Is the Key* (Portfolio/Penguin, 2019), 215.

"the need to connect with others..." E.S. Buchholz, *The Call of Solitude: Alone Time in a World of Attachment* (Simon & Schuster, 1997).

"also allows you to have fresher ideas..." M. Harris, *Solitude: In Pursuit of a Singular Life in a Crowded World* (Thomas Dunne, 2017).

"'promotes self-understanding...'" A. Storr, *Solitude: A Return to the Self* (Free Press, 1988, 2005), 40.

"'filter out the inconsequential.'" Holiday, *Stillness,* 31.

"Nate Fick, a former Marine Recon officer..." R.M. Kethledge and M.S. Erwin, *Lead Yourself First: Inspiring Leadership Through Solitude* (Bloomsbury USA, 2017).

"compared journaling to windshield wipers..." J. Cameron, *The Artist's Way Morning Pages Journal: A Companion Volume to the Artist's Way* (Tarcher Perigee, 1997).

"questions that start with 'why...'" Eurich, "Really Is."

"thinking about why one is..." J.G. Hixon and W.B. Swann, "When Does Introspection Bear Fruit? Self-Reflection, Self-Insight, and Interpersonal Choices," *Journal of Personality and Social Psychology* 64, no. 1 (1993): 35–43, 40, doi.org/10.1037/0022-3514.64.1.35.

"consider reflecting on questions such as..." Holiday, *Stillness.*

"Eisenhower's journaling allowed him..." Kethledge and Erwin, *Lead Yourself.*

"The advantage that walking provides..." F. Gros, *A Philosophy of Walking* (Verso, 2014).

"'Helicopter rides were...'" Kethledge and Erwin, *Lead Yourself,* 10.

"if they want to be in the top 5 percent..." G. Robinson, interview with author, 2018.

"'When leaders tell me they're way...'" K.N. Lawrence, *Your Oxygen Mask First: 17 Habits to Help High Achievers Survive & Thrive in Leadership & Life* (Lioncrest, 2017), 110.

"Neil Pasricha recommends several..." N. Pasricha, "8 Ways to Read (a Lot) More Books This Year," *Harvard Business Review,* February 3, 2017, hbr.org/2017/02/8-ways-to-read-a-lot-more-books-this-year.

"the top performing leaders read..." B. Smart and G. Smart, *Topgrading: How to Hire, Coach and Keep A Players* (Pritchett, 2005).

"'If you finish a book...'" Lawrence, *Oxygen,* 117.

"During these seven days in solitude..." R.A. Guth, "In Secret Hideaway, Bill Gates Ponders Microsoft's Future," *Wall Street Journal,* March 28, 2005, wsj.com/articles/SB111196625830690477.

"your performance will improve..." G. Di Stefano, F. Gino, G. Pisano, and B.R. Staats, "Making Experience Count: The Role of Reflection in Individual Learning," Harvard Business School NOM Unit Working Paper No. 14-093; Harvard Business School Technology & Operations Mgt. Unit Working Paper No. 14-093; HEC Paris Research Paper No. SPE-2016-1181, June 14, 2016, dx.doi.org/10.2139/ssrn.2414478.

"Solitude enables you to obtain..." Kethledge and Erwin, *Lead Yourself.*

"'When you practice stillness...'" R. Holiday, email exchange with author, 2020.

"Like many people I started..." H.M. Kraemer, *From Values to Action: The Four Principles of Values-Based Leadership* (Jossey-Bass, 2011), 59.

"honest self-reflection will likely cause..." Holiday, *Ego.*

"questions to ask yourself include..." Hougaard and Carter, *Mind of the Leader.*

"people who are more humble in nature..." C.C. Banker and M.R. Leary, "Hypo-Egoic Nonentitlement as a Feature of Humility," *Personality and Social Psychology Bulletin* 46, no. 5 (2019): 738–53, doi.org/10.1177/014616 7219875144.

"like sweeping the floor in a dusty room..." Holiday, *Ego.*

Chapter 6: Vulnerability

" 'Jan has a great connection...' " J. Wyllie, email exchange with author, 2020.

" 'This is the place from which...' " Kaffer, interview with author, 2019.

"She has a rule to not tweet..." D. Corbet, "The Healthcare CEO Keeping Things Real on Social Media," The Social C-Suite, July 15, 2018, thesocialcsuite.net/janice-kaffer-healthcare-ceo-social-media.

" 'the purpose of all these values...' " C. Argyris, "Teaching Smart People How to Learn," *Harvard Business Review* (May–June 1991), 6.

"convinced themselves of 'the myth...' " D. Ancona, T.W. Malone, W.J. Orlikowski, and P.M. Senge, "In Praise of the Incomplete Leader," *Harvard Business Review* (February 2007), hbr.org/2007/02/in-praise-of-the-incomplete-leader

" 'embracing an appropriate fallibility...' " Hoekstra, Bell, and Peterson, "Abandoning," 14.

" 'I came clean and I told...' " Jones, interview with author, 2019.

"Brown defined vulnerability..." B. Brown, *Dare to Lead: Brave Work, Tough Conversations, Whole Hearts* (Random House, 2018).

"Brown explains that healthy striving..." B. Brown, *The Gifts of Imperfection* (Simon & Schuster, 2010).

" 'If I had one wish...' " E. Holmes, "Elizabeth Holmes, Theranos CEO at TedMed 2014," MedCity News, September 12, 2014, YouTube video, 2:04, youtube.com/watch?v=ho8geEtcYjw&ab_channel=MedCityNews.

"She often claimed that her uncle's..." B. Read, "The Inventor Misses Elizabeth Holmes's—And Silicon Valley's—Most Insidious Crimes," *Vogue*, March 19, 2019, vogue.com/article/the-inventor-hbo-theranos-elizabeth-holmes-alex-gibney-documentary-review.

"the unreliable results..." J. Carreyrou, *Bad Blood: Secrets and Lies in a Silicon Valley Startup* (Knopf, 2018).

"published a series of long articles..." M. Hixenbaugh, "Heart Failure," *Houston Chronicle*, May 16, 2018, houstonchronicle.com/news/ investigations/article/Heart-Failure-patients-suffer-at-St-Lukes-Houston-12916224.php.

" 'I didn't realize how bad...' " D. Lawson, interview with author, 2019.

" 'When I recently stepped into...' " D. Lawson, "Open Letter from Doug Lawson," St. Luke's Health, February 26, 2019, stlukeshealth.org/ newsroom/open-letter-doug-lawson-ph-d-o.

"U.S. Navy SEAL officers..." J. Willink and L. Babin, *Extreme Ownership: How U.S. Navy SEALs Lead and Win* (St. Martin's Press, 2017).

"Humble people are less inclined..." P.D. Dunlop, K. Lee, M.C. Ashton, S.B. Butcher, and A. Dykstra, "Please Accept My Sincere and Humble Apologies: The HEXACO Model of Personality and the Proclivity to Apologize," *Personality and Individual Differences* 79 (2015): 140–45, sciencedirect.com/science/article/abs/pii/S0191886915000963.

" 'I'm serious, because one of the things...' " T. Coates, "Imagining a New America," November 16, 2017, *On Being*, hosted by Krista Tippett, podcast, MP3 audio, 52:35, onbeing.org/programs/ ta-nehisi-coates-imagining-a-new-america.

"they respond by bringing..." Hoekstra, Bell, and Peterson, "Abandoning."

" 'Each year I created...' " J. Cohn, "Why CEOs Should Model Vulnerability," *Harvard Business Review*, May 11, 2020, hbr.org/2020/05/why-ceos-should-model-vulnerability.

" 'You can imagine all of the fears...' " Cohn, "Why CEOs," 4.

"he didn't last longer..." Angus, interview with author.

"it requires a 'unique sort...' " Owens, Johnson, and Mitchell, "Expressed Humility."

" 'ordinary courage is about...' " Brown, *Gifts*.

"In order to model this behavior..." C. Tavris and E. Aronson, *Mistakes Were Made (But Not by Me)* (Harcourt, 2015).

"psychological phenomenon that takes place..." Tavris and Aronson, *Mistakes*.

"to overcome cognitive dissonance..." Tavris and Aronson, *Mistakes*.

"Imagine this experiment..." A. Arun, E. Melinat, E. Aron, R.D. Vallone, and R.J. Bator, "The Experimental Generation of Interpersonal Closeness: A Procedure and Some Preliminary Findings," *Personality and Social Psychology Bulletin* 23, no. 4 (1997): 363–77.

"These conversations appeared..." F. Meyer, D.M. Le Fevre, and V.M.J. Robinson, "How Leaders Communicate Their Vulnerability: Implications for Trust Building," *International Journal of Educational Management* 31, no. 2 (2017): 221-35, 230, doi.org/10.1108/IJEM-11-2015-0150.

"leaders who act in this way..." A. Ito and M. Bligh, "Feeling Vulnerable? Disclosure of Vulnerability in the Charismatic Leadership Relationship," *Journal of Leadership Studies* 10, no. 3 (2016): 66-70, doi.org/10.1002/jls.21492.

"results in those team members..." E. Seppälä, "What Bosses Gain by Being Vulnerable," *Harvard Business Review*, December 11, 2014, hbr.org/2014/12/what-bosses-gain-by-being-vulnerable.

"Even a superficial apology..." A. Brooks, H. Dai, and M. Schweitzer, "I'm Sorry about the Rain! Superfluous Apologies Demonstrate Empathic Concern and Increase Trust," *Social Psychological and Personality Science* 5, no. 4 (2013): 467-74, journals.sagepub.com/doi/10.1177/1948550613506122.

"researchers asked people to read..." J. Robbenholt, "Apologies and Settlement Levers," *Journal of Empirical Legal Studies* 3 (2006): 333, doi.org/10.1111/j.1740-1461.2006.00072.x.

"'It's got to be safe...'" D. Coyle, *The Culture Code: The Secrets of Highly Success-ful Groups* (Bantam Books, 2018), 140-41.

"'This new normal...'" G. Burnison, "It's Time to Be Vulnerable," Korn Ferry, 2020, kornferry.com/insights/articles/vulnerability-leadership-coronavirus.

"Although higher status individuals..." K. Gibson, D. Harari, and J. Marr, "When Sharing Hurts: How and Why Self-Disclosing Weakness Under-mines the Task-Oriented Relationships of Higher Status Disclosers," *Organizational Behavior and Human Decision Processes* 144 (2018): 25-43, 38, dx.doi.org/10.1016/j.obhdp.2017.09.001.

"'I want to do this job...'" H. Ibarra, "The Authenticity Paradox," *Harvard Business Review* (January–February 2015), 4, hbr.org/2015/01/the-authenticity-paradox.

"Once you have established..." A. Grant, "Authenticity Is a Double-Edged Sword," April 6, 2020, TED, *WorkLife With Adam Grant*, podcast, 38:15, ted.com/talks/worklife_with_adam_grant_authenticity_is_a_double_edged_sword?language=en.

"sends a message of empathy..." Brown, *Dare to Lead*.

"delicate balance required in bringing…" R. Goffee and G. Jones, "Managing Authenticity," *Harvard Business Review* (December 2005), hbr.org/2005/12/managing-authenticity-the-paradox-of-great-leadership.

Chapter 7: Open-Mindedness

"bloodiest single day in history…" A. Zamoyski, *Moscow 1812: Napoleon's Fatal March* (Harper Perennial, 2004, 2005).

"a mere 20,000 of his men were alive…" M.J. Kroll, L.A. Toombs, and P. Wright, "Napoleon's Tragic March Home from Moscow: Lessons in Hubris," *Academy of Management Executive* 14, no. 1 (2000): 117–28.

"'Napoleon, supreme egoist…'" M. De Fezensac, *The Russian Campaign*, trans. L. Kennett, (University of Georgia Press [1812], 1970), viii.

"He was extremely thin-skinned…" A. Zamoyski, "The Personality Traits That Led to Napoleon Bonaparte's Epic Downfall," *History*, April 9, 2019, history.com/news/napoleon-bonaparte-downfall-reasons-personality-traits.

"Infatuated by Roman emperors from…" A. Knighton, "Napoleon as Augustus: How He Modelled Himself on the Roman Empire," War History Online, February 26, 2016, warhistoryonline.com/ancient-history/napoleon-as-augustus.html.

"'One good battle will…'" Kroll, Toombs, and Wright, "Tragic March," 122.

"'Thanks to Napoleon's…'" R. Zaretsky, "Napoleon Wrote the Best Political Memoir," *Politico Magazine*, June 17, 2015, politico.com/magazine/story/2015/06/napoleon-bonaparte-wrote-best-political-memoir-waterloo-119115.

"you need to be willing to change…" J. Spiegel, "Open-Mindedness and Intellectual Humility," *Theory and Research in Education* 10, no. 1 (2012): 27–38, journals.sagepub.com/doi/10.1177/1477878512437472.

"knowing what you know…" S.A. Deffler, M.R. Leary, and R.H. Hoyle, "Knowing What You Know: Intellectual Humility and Judgements of Recognition Memory," *Personality and Individual Differences* 96 (2016): 255–59.

"'he doesn't claim to know…'" T. Porter, "Intellectual Humility," Character Lab, characterlab.org/playbooks/intellectual-humility/endnotes.

"to determine people's tendency…" Deffler, Leary, and Hoyle, "Knowing What."

"asks people to rate themselves…" M.R. Leary, K.J. Diebels, E.K. Davisson, K.P. Jongman-Sereno, J.C. Isherwood, K.T. Raimi, S.A. Deffler, and R.H.

Hoyle, "Cognitive and Interpersonal Features of Intellectual Humility," *Personality and Social Psychology Bulletin* 43, no. 6 (2017): 793–813.

"intellectual humility enables..." Deffler, Leary, and Hoyle, "Knowing What."

"those who displayed intellectual humility..." T. Porter, "Intellectual Humility, Mindset, and Learning" (PhD diss., Stanford University, 2015), coa. stanford.edu/publications/intellectual-humility-mindset-and-learning.

"review of the expanding literature..." Porter, "Intellectual Humility."

"In a third-grade classroom..." T. Porter, "The Benefits of Admitting When You Don't Know," *Behavioral Scientist*, April 30, 2018, behavioralscientist. org/the-benefits-of-admitting-when-you-dont-know.

"The children were asked to assess..." J.H. Danovitch, M. Fisher, H. Schroder, D.Z. Hambrick, and J. Moser, "Intelligence and Neurophysiological Markers of Error Monitoring Relate to Children's Intellectual Humility," *Child Development* 90, no. 3 (2019): 924–39, doi.org/10.1111/cdev. 12960.

"intellectually humble kids are more motivated..." Porter, "Benefits of Admitting."

"a group of ten- and eleven-year-olds..." S. Hagá and K.R. Olson, "'If I Only Had a Little Humility, I Would Be Perfect': Children's and Adults' Perceptions of Intellectually Arrogant, Humble, and Diffident People," *Journal of Positive Psychology* 12, no. 1 (2017): 87–98, doi.org/10.1080/17 439760.2016.1167943.

"I actually did vote..." J. Roberts, "Kerry's Top Ten Flip-Flops," CBS News, September 29, 2004, cbsnews.com/news/kerrys-top-ten-flip-flops.

"more likely to believe that politicians..." Leary et al., "Features."

"We've all met them..." T.M. Nichols, *The Death of Expertise: The Campaign Against Established Knowledge and Why It Matters* (Oxford University Press, 2019), 13.

"'while there has probably never...'" F.T. McAndrew, "Could a Lack of Humility Be at the Root of What Ails America?" *The Conversation*, May 23, 2019, theconversation.com/could-a-lack-of-humility-be-at-the-root-of-what-ails-america-116118.

"'The test of open-mindedness...'" W. Hare, "Open-Mindedness in Moral Education: Three Contemporary Approaches," *Journal of Moral Education* 16, no. 2 (1987): 99–107, 99.

"means a willingness to subject..." Spiegel, "Intellectual Humility."

"'I forbid myself...'" Franklin, *Autobiography*, 42.

"Franklin aimed to start..." S. Snow, "A New Way to Become More Open-Minded," *Harvard Business Review*, November 20, 2018, hbr.org/2018/ 11/a-new-way-to-become-more-open-minded.

"the other person has lost..." K. Murphy, *You're Not Listening: What You're Missing and Why It Matters* (Celadon Books, 2020).

"In a survey of 1,500..." S. Harrison, "83% of Executives Say They Encourage Curiosity," *Harvard Business Review*, September 20, 2018, hbr.org/2018/09/research-83-of-executives-say-they-encourage-curiosity-just-52-of-employees-agree.

"40 percent of our questions..." Hess and Ludwig, *New Smart.*

"A high questions-to-statements ratio..." Hoekstra, Bell, and Peterson, "Abandoning."

" 'the fine art of drawing...' " E.H. Schein, *Humble Inquiry: The Gentle Art of Asking Instead of Telling* (Berrett-Koehler Books, 2013), 21.

" 'know your voice isn't the only...' " M. Bungay Stanier, *The Advice Trap* (Page Two, 2020), 55.

"the best questions for a leader to ask..." M. Bungay Stanier, *The Coaching Habit: Say Less, Ask More & Change the Way You Lead Forever* (Page Two, 2016).

"to decrease your talking time..." Hoekstra, Bell, and Peterson, "Abandoning."

"great listeners do not act like a sponge..." J. Zenger and J. Folkman, "What Great Listeners Actually Do," *Harvard Business Review*, July 14, 2016, hbr.org/2016/07/what-great-listeners-actually-do.

"keep it in regular mode..." Murphy, *Not Listening.*

"most of us spend 60 percent..." C. Headlee, *We Need to Talk: How to Have Conversations That Matter* (Harper Wave, 2017).

"most people listen to reply..." S. Covey, *The 7 Habits of Highly Effective People* (Free Press, 1989).

"take a moment or two to think..." Murphy, *Not Listening.*

" 'For me, a humble leader...' " D. Anderson, interview with author, 2019.

" 'If you have an obligation...' " B. Taylor, "True Leaders Believe Dissent Is an Obligation," *Harvard Business Review*, January 12, 2017, hbr.org/2017/01/true-leaders-believe-dissent-is-an-obligation.

"Leader humility at the most basic..." Owens and Hekman, "How to Grow."

"which inevitably leads to learning..." Dweck, *Mindset.*

"active empathetic listening leads to better..." C. Gearhart and C. Bodie, "Active-Empathic Listening as a General Social Skill: Evidence from Bivariate and Canonical Correlations," *Communication Reports* 24, no. 2 (2011): 86–98, tandfonline.com/doi/abs/10.1080/08934215.2011.610731.

"results in increased learning capacity..." M. Lord, "Group Learning Capacity: The Roles of Open-Mindedness and Shared Vision," *Frontiers in Psychology* 6, no. 1322 (2015): 150, researchgate.net/publication/

273638631_Group_learning_capacity_The_roles_of_open-mindedness_
and_shared_vision.

"and to better job satisfaction..." R. van den Bosch and T.W. Taris, "Authenticity at Work: Development and Validation of an Individual Authenticity
Measure at Work," *Journal of Happiness Studies* 15, no. 1 (2014): 1–18, doi.
org/10.1007/s10902-013-9413-3.

"they are less dogmatic..." A. Homan, "Facing Differences with an Open
Mind: Openness to Experience, Salience of Intragroup Differences,
and Performance of Diverse Work Groups," *Academy of Management
Journal* 51, no. 6 (2008): 1204–22, journals.aom.org/doi/full/10.5465/
amj.2008.35732995.

Chapter 8: Appreciation

"and he soon received an offer..." D. Stachowiak, "How to Create Leadership
Connections in the Smallest of Moments with TouchPoints from
Douglas Conant," *Coaching for Leaders,* podcast, episode 136, 48:06,
coachingforleaders.com/podcast/touchpoints.

"'I wanted them to know...'"; "'What I found is...'" S. Melamed, "Gratitude
Tips from the Author of 30,000 Thank-you Notes," *Philadelphia Inquirer*,
November 24, 2016, inquirer.com/philly/living/Thanksgiving-pro-tips-
from-the-author-of-30000-thank-you-notes.html.

"he put his sneakers on..." D. Conant and M. Norgaard, *TouchPoints: Creating
Powerful Leadership Connections in the Smallest of Moments* (Jossey-Bass,
2011).

"'As my wife and I...'" D. Conant, "Secrets of Positive Feedback," *Harvard
Business Review*, February 16, 2011, hbr.org/2011/02/secrets-of-positive-
feedback.

"'What unifies expressions of gratitude...'" D. DeSteno, *Emotional Success: The
Power of Gratitude, Compassion, and Pride* (Houghton Mifflin Harcourt,
2018), 58.

"there is a significant gap between..." K. Gibson, K. O'Leary, and J. Weintraub,
"The Little Things That Make Employees Feel Appreciated," *Harvard
Business Review*, January 23, 2020, hbr.org/2020/01/the-little-things-
that-make-employees-feel-appreciated.

"while 88 percent of CEOs believe..." Thnks, "90% of CEOs Claim to Lead
with Gratitude while Only 37% of Employees Are Satisfied with the
Appreciation They Receive," Cision PR Newswire, January 29, 2019,

prnewswire.com/news-releases/survey-90-of-ceos-claim-to-lead-with-gratitude-while-only-37-of-employees-are-satisfied-with-the-appreciation-they-receive-300785710.html.

"recognition is about what people do..." M. Robbins, "Why Employees Need Both Recognition and Appreciation," *Harvard Business Review,* November 12, 2019, hbr.org/2019/11/why-employees-need-both-recognition-and-appreciation.

"an 'attitude of gratitude' is an integral part..." T.S. Chiu, H.J. Huang, and Y. Hung, "The Influence of Humility on Leadership: A Chinese and Western Review," *International Proceedings of Economics Development and Research* 29, no. 24 (2012): 129-33.

"appreciation—affirming others' value..." M.A. Hayes and M. Comer, *Start with Humility: Lessons from America's Quiet CEOs on How to Build Trust and Inspire Followers* (Greenleaf Center for Servant Leadership, 2010).

"a practice called 'the window...'" Collins, *Good to Great.*

"there is a 'mutually reinforcing...'" E. Kruse, J. Chancellor, P.M. Ruberton, and S. Lyubomirsky, "An Upward Spiral Between Gratitude and Humility," *Social Psychological and Personality Science* 5, no. 7 (2014): 805-14, doi.org/10.1177/1948550614534700.

"'I try to write as many...'" Anderson, interview with author.

"the habit of sending thank-you notes..." Q. Studer, *Hardwiring Excellence: Purpose, Worthwhile Work, Making a Difference* (Fire Starter, 2003).

"reported feeling more happiness..." S.M. Toepfer, K. Cichy, and P. Peters, "Letters of Gratitude: Further Evidence for Author Benefits," *Journal of Happiness Studies* 13, no. 1 (2012): 187-201, doi.org/10.1007/s10902-011-9257-7.

"were more likely to engage..." C. Armenta, M. Fritz, and S. Lyubomirsky, "Functions of Positive Emotions," *Emotion Review* 9, no. 3 (2016), doi.org/10.1177/175407391666959.

"'I know how this works...'" R.A. Eckert, "The Two Most Important Words," *Harvard Business Review* (April 2013), hbr.org/2013/04/the-two-most-important-words.

"'Is there anyone you would like...'" Studer, *Hardwiring Excellence.*

"advises leaders to adopt in order to remain..." D. Keltner, "Don't Let Power Corrupt You," *Harvard Business Review* (October 2016), hbr.org/2016/10/dont-let-power-corrupt-you.

"teams whose players touched..." M.W. Kraus, C. Huang, and D. Keltner, "Tactile Communication, Cooperation, and Performance: An Ethological Study of the NBA," *Emotion* 10, no. 5 (2010): 745-49, doi.org/10.1037/a0019382.

"the other person becomes more responsive..." H. Grant, "Stop Making Gratitude All About You," *Harvard Business Review*, June 29, 2016, hbr.org/2016/06/stop-making-gratitude-all-about-you.

"you could grab a book you think..." Hayes and Comer, *Start with Humility*.

"'Gratitude promotes the savoring...'" S. Lyubomirsky, D. Schkade, and K. Sheldon, "Pursuing Happiness: The Architecture of Sustainable Change," *Review of General Psychology* 9, no. 2 (2005): 111-31, journals.sagepub.com/doi/10.1037/1089-2680.9.2.111.

"such as a stronger immune system..." R. Emmons, *Thanks!: How Practicing Gratitude Can Make You Happier* (Mariner Books, 2008).

"more likely to provide assistance..." M. Bartlett and D. DeSteno, "Gratitude and Prosocial Behavior," *Psychological Science* 17, no. 4 (2006): 319-25, doi.org/10.1111/j.1467-9280.2006.01705.x.

"step in building long-term relationships..." M. Bartlett, P. Condon, J. Cruz, J. Baumann, and D. DeSteno, "Gratitude: Prompting Behaviours That Build Relationships," *Cognition and Emotion* 26, no. 1 (2011): 2-13, doi.org/10.1080/02699931.2011.561297.

"You develop more patience..." D. DeSteno, "Gratitude: A Tool for Reducing Economic Impatience," *Psychological Science* 25, no. 6 (2014): 1262-67, journals.sagepub.com/doi/10.1177/0956797614529979.

"66 percent of the participants who received..." A. Grant, "A Little Thanks Goes a Long Way: Explaining Why Gratitude Expressions Motivate Prosocial Behavior," *Journal of Personality and Social Psychology* 98, no. 6 (2010): 946-55, pubmed.ncbi.nlm.nih.gov/20515249.

"'The LinkedIn data shows...'" WorkHuman, "Gratitude and Recognition," hub.workhuman.com/gratitude-recognition-1.

"recognition leading to improved commitment..." P. Gohari, A. Kamkar, S.J. Hosseinipour, and M. Zohoori, "Relationship between Rewards and Employee Performance: A Mediating Role of Job Satisfaction," *Interdisciplinary Journal of Contemporary Research in Business* 5, no. 3 (2013): 571-97.

"better team performance..." P. Geue, "Positive Practices in the Workplace: Impact on Team Climate, Work Engagement, and Task Performance," *Emerging Leadership Journeys* 10, no. 1 (2017): 70-99, journals.sagepub.com/doi/abs/10.1177/0021886318773459.

"'I have to say that the single...'" O. Winfrey, "Harvard Commencement Speech," Harvard University, May 30, 2013, YouTube video, 28:58, youtube.com/watch?v=GMWFieBGR7c&ab_channel=HarvardUniversity.

Chapter 9: Generosity

"*I love to hear the cash registers...*'" J. Chu, "CEO Interview: Costco's Jim Sinegal," *Fast Company*, November 1, 2008, fastcompany.com/1042487/ceo-interview-costcos-jim-sinegal.

"*a little nook that had no door...*" J. McGregor, "The Costco Kings Checks Out," *Washington Post*, September 2, 2011, washingtonpost.com/blogs/post-leadership/post/costco-ceo-jim-sinegal-checks- out/2011/04/01/gIQAh7CqwJ_blog.html.

"'*I don't see what's wrong...*'" J. Flanigan, "Costco Sees Value in Higher Pay," *LA Times*, February 15, 2004, latimes.com/archives/la-xpm-2004-feb-15-fi-flan15-story.html.

"'*arrogance is a like a cancer...*'" M. Gist, *The Extraordinary Power of Leader Humility: Thriving Organizations & Great Results* (Berrett-Koehler, 2020), 22.

"*participants listen to an audio recording...*" J.P. LaBouff, W.C. Rowatt, M.K. Johnson, J.-A. Tsang, and G.M. Willerton, "Humble Persons Are More Helpful Than Less Humble Persons: Evidence from Three Studies," *Journal of Positive Psychology* 7, no. 1 (2012): 16–29, doi.org/10.1080/17439760.2011.626787.

"*humble people reported greater motives...*" J.J. Exline and P.C. Hill, "Humility: A Consistent and Robust Predictor of Generosity," *Journal of Positive Psychology* 7, no. 3 (2012): 208–18, doi.org/10.1080/17439760.2012.671348.

"*they had an unwavering commitment...*" Collins, *Good to Great*.

"'*I need your collaboration...*'" Hoekstra, Bell, and Peterson, "Abandoning," 20.

"*give from their time...*" A.M. Grant, *Give and Take: Why Helping Others Drives Our Success* (Viking, 2014).

"*as a 'tendency to feel and display...*'" Gist, *Extraordinary Power*, xv.

"*one-year-olds whose parents...*" J. Zaki, *The War for Kindness: Building Empathy in a Fractured World* (Crown, 2019).

"*this region is typically associated...*" C. Hutcherson, B. Bushon, and A. Rangel, "A Neurocomputational Model of Altruistic Choice and Its Implications," *Neuron* 87, no. 2 (2015): 451–62, pubmed.ncbi.nlm.nih.gov/26182424.

"*you can be 'compassionately competitive...*'" M. Ross, *The Empathy Edge: Harnessing the Value of Compassion as an Engine for Success* (Page Two, 2019), 1.

"*it actually requires the strength...*" Hougaard and Carter, *Mind of the Leader*.

"Through practice, we can grow…" Zaki, *War for Kindness*, 15.

"that are intended to help your followers…" D. Dierendonck, "Compassionate Love as a Cornerstone of Servant Leadership," *Journal of Business Ethics* 128, no. 1 (2015): 119-31, link.springer.com/article/10.1007%2Fs10551-014-2085-z.

"Elegantly simple, yet extremely…'"; *"'Don't let all the brilliance…'"* J. Glickman, "Be Generous at Work," *Harvard Business Review*, June 8, 2011, hbr.org/2011/06/be-generous-at-work.

"You need to show your team members…" B. Bonner, *Inspiring Generosity* (Wisdom Publications, 2014).

"you ought to open the door…" "13 Characteristics of a Generous Leader," Vanderbloemen, May 12, 2014, vanderbloemen.com/blog/13-characteristics-of-a-generous-leader.

"who tends to succeed more at work…" Grant, *Give and Take*.

"professional engineers in California rated…" F. Flynn, "How Much Should I Give and How Often?" *Academy of Management Journal* 46, no. 5 (2003): 539-53, jstor.org/stable/30040648.

"a study conducted at Belgian medical…" F. Lievens, D. Ones, and S. Dilchert, "Personality Scale Validities Increase Throughout Medical School," *Journal of Applied Psychology* 94, no. 6 (2009): 1514-35, pubmed.ncbi.nlm.nih.gov/19916659.

"Generosity appear[s] to sink…" A. Grant, "In the Company of Givers and Takers," *Harvard Business Review* (April 2013), hbr.org/2013/04/in-the-company-of-givers-and-takers.

"typically taken advantage of by others…" C. Nickisch, "Leaders Who Get How to Give," *Harvard Business Review*, January 24, 2017, hbr.org/2017/01/leaders-who-get-how-to-give.

"When you don't create enemies…" Grant, *Give and Take*.

"will feel they have access…" M. Thomas, "4 Ways Leaders Can Protect Their Time and Empower Their Teams," *Harvard Business Review*, July 18, 2018, hbr.org/2018/07/4-ways-leaders-can-protect-their-time-and-empower-their-teams.

"if you know how to manage…" A. Rapp, "The Influence of Time Management Skill on the Curvilinear Relationship between Organizational Citizenship Behavior and Task Performance," *Journal of Applied Psychology* 98, no. 4 (2013): 668-77, psycnet.apa.org/record/2013-03481-001.

"leaders have the unique…'" Grant, "Company of Givers."

"spending without putting money in…" Grant, *Give and Take*.

"That day on the bus..." Nickisch, "Leaders Who Get."

"Leadership amounts to wanting..." B. Herrera, *The Gift of Struggle: Life-Changing Lessons about Leading* (Bard Press, 2019).

"the more you help and develop..." M. Tsvetkova and M. Macy, "The Social Contagion of Generosity," *PLOS One* 9, no. 2 (2013): e87275, doi. org/10.1371/journal.pone.0087275.

"You shine a spotlight on them..." L. Wiseman and G. McKeown, *Multipliers: How the Best Leaders Make Everyone Smarter* (Harper Business, 2010).

"when people are part of a more..." E. Nook, D.C. Ong, S.A. Morelli, J.P. Mitchell, and J. Zaki, "Prosocial Conformity: Prosocial Norms Generalize across Behavior and Empathy," *Personality and Social Psychology Bulletin* 42, no. 8 (2016): 1045-62, journals.sagepub.com/ doi/10.1177/0146167216649932.

"what gets modeled gets repeated..." F. Gino and A.D. Galinsky, "Vicarious Dishonesty: When Psychological Closeness Creates Distance from One's Moral Compass," *Organizational Behavior and Human Decision Processes* 119, no. 1 (2012): 15-26, doi.org/10.1016/j.obhdp.2012.03.011.

"when employees are involved in opportunities..." C. Riordan, "Foster a Culture of Gratitude," *Harvard Business Review*, April 23, 2013, hbr.org/2013/04/ foster-a-culture-of-gratitude.

"asked the CFOs of technology organizations..." S. Peterson, B. Galvin, and D. Lange, "CEO Servant Leadership: Exploring Executive Characteristics and Firm Performance," *Personnel Psychology* 65 (2012): 565-96, 589, doi.org/10.1111/j.1744-6570.2012.01253.x.

"The best role model of humility..." D. Lubetzky, interview with author, 2019.

"I'd rather make the mistake..." D. Lubetzky, *Do the KIND Thing: Think Boundlessly, Work Purposefully, Live Passionately* (Ballantine, 2015), 210.

"His entire story..." Lubetzky, *KIND Thing*, 203.

"If we were at a restaurant..." Lubetzky, interview with author, 2019.

"The company then sends..." Lubetzky, *KIND Thing*.

"one of the most successful companies..." C. Fairchild, "Why Kind Bars Are Suddenly Everywhere," *Fortune*, February 10, 2014, fortune. com/2014/02/10/why-kind-bars-are-suddenly-everywhere.

"people who give more social support..." R. Piferi and K. Lawler, "Social Support and Ambulatory Blood Pressure: An Examination of Both Receiving and Giving," *International Journal of Psychophysiology* 62, no. 2 (2006): 328-36, sciencedirect.com/science/article/abs/pii/ S0167876006001917.

"these are the same centers..." W. Harbaugh, U. Mayr, and D. Burghart, "Neural Responses to Taxation and Voluntary Giving Reveal Motives for Charitable Donations," *Science* 316, no. 5831 (2007): 1622-25, pubmed. ncbi.nlm.nih.gov/17569866.

"'human beings around the world experience...'"; *"people who gave money to charity felt happier..."* L. Aknin, C.P. Barrington-Leigh, E.W. Dunn, J.F. Helliwell, J. Burns, R. Biswas-Diener, I. Kemeza, P. Nyende, C.E. Ashton-James, and M.I. Norton, "Prosocial Spending and Well-Being: Cross-Cultural Evidence for a Psychological Universal," *Journal of Personality and Social Psychology* 104, no. 4 (2013): 635-52, 546, doi. org/10.1037/a0031578.

"participants reflected on times..." L. Aknin, "Making a Difference Matters," *Journal of Economic Behavior and Organization* 88 (2013): 90-95, doi. org/10.1016/j.jebo.2013.01.008.

"positive effects of giving on reducing mortality risks..." M.J. Poulin, S.L. Brown, A.J. Dillard, and D.M. Smith, "Giving to Others and the Association between Stress and Mortality," *American Journal of Public Health* 103, no. 9 (2013): 1649-55, ajph.aphapublications.org/doi/10.2105/AJPH. 2012.300876.

"'Doing this lets you do...'" M. Gill and T. Roulet, "Stressed at Work? Mentoring a Colleague Could Help," *Harvard Business Review*, March 1, 2019, hbr.org/2019/03/stressed-at-work-mentoring-a-colleague-could-help.

"when you offer unsolicited help..." A. Beard, "You Shouldn't Volunteer to Help Your Coworkers," *Harvard Business Review* (March-April 2019), hbr. org/2019/03/you-shouldnt-volunteer-to-help-your-coworkers.

Chapter 10: Transcendence

"he often referred to himself..." R. Wiedeman, *Billion Dollar Loser: The Epic Rise and Spectacular Fall of Adam Neumann and WeWork* (Little, Brown and Company, 2020).

"'the influence and impact...'" E. Brown, "How Adam Neumann's Over-the-Top Style Built WeWork: 'This Is Not the Way Everybody Behaves,'" *Wall Street Journal*, September 18, 2019, wsj.com/articles/this-is-not-the-way-everybody-behaves-how-adam-neumanns-over-the-top-style-built-wework-11568823827.

"combined this "brash self-promotion..." W. Kirn, "The Cautionary Tale of Adam Neumann and WeWork," *New York Times*, October 23, 2020,

nytimes.com/2020/10/23/books/review/billion-dollar-loser-adam-neumann-wework-reeves-wiedeman.html.

"Neumann arrogantly responded..." A. Hartmans, "Former Starbucks CEO Howard Schultz Once Reportedly Advised Adam Neumann to Stop Growing WeWork So Quickly and Fix Its Problems. Neumann Responded 'F--- That,'" *Business Insider*, October 24, 2020, businessinsider.com/adam-neumann-rejected-howard-schultz-starbucks-wework-advice-2020-10.

"'I am young and unknown...'" R. Basler, ed., *The Collected Works of Abraham Lincoln*, vol. V: *1861–1862* (Rutgers University Press, 1953).

"your humble behaviors may not be sustainable..." Ou et al., "Connections to Top Management."

"you start to realize that you are not..." Tangney, "Humility: Theoretical Perspectives."

"'A narcissist can be happy...'" D. Brooks, *The Second Mountain: The Quest for a Moral Life* (Random House, 2019), xxiv.

"transcendent leaders rise above..." G. Stebbins, *Transcendent Leadership: Manifesting Organizational Vitality* (Savvy Books, 2020).

"'If a leader is being humble...'" G. Stebbins, email exchange with author, 2020.

"your main thinking shifts from selfish..." E. Brooks and B. Willis, "Introducing the Humility Gap," The Oxford Character Project, SoundCloud, soundcloud.com/haracterroject/interview-introduction-to-the-humility-gap-podcast-series.

"to uncover the importance of leader connectedness..." Wang et al., "Affective Impact."

"wanted to understand the specific experiences..." M. Morse, "A Quality of Interrelating: Describing a Form of Meaningful Experience on a Wilderness River Journey," *Journal of Adventure Education and Outdoor Learning* 14, no. 1 (2013): 42–55, doi.org/10.1080/14729679.2013.769713.

"'When you stop and you look...'" Morse, "Quality of Interrelating," 47.

"'The sense of diminishment...'" Morse, "Quality of Interrelating," 49.

"They acknowledge their status as..." Havard, *Created for Greatness.*

"And on the pedestal..." D.H. Reiman, ed., *Shelley's Poetry and Prose: Authoritative Texts, Criticism* (W.W. Norton, 1977).

"'There is no greater reminder...'" Stulberg and Magness, *Passion Paradox*, 138.

"you can reflect on the following..." Stulberg and Magness, *Passion Paradox*, 139–40.

"can lead to reflections..." D.R. Vago and D.A. Silbersweig, "Self-Awareness, Self-Regulation, and Self-Transcendence (S-ART): A Framework for

Understanding the Neurobiological Mechanisms of Mindfulness,"
Frontiers in Human Neuroscience 6 (2012): 296, doi.org/10.3389/
fnhum.2012.00296.
"taking a few breaths in and out…'" M. Birk, "What Meditation Can Do for
Your Leadership," *Harvard Business Review*, December 6, 2019, hbr.
org/2019/12/what-meditation-can-do-for-your-leadership.
"'Ego blocks us from the beauty…'" Holiday, Ego, 139–40.
"You see yourself accurately…" Morris, Brotheridge, and Urbanski, "Bringing
Humility."
"'Regardless of how substantial…'" B. Treasurer, *The Leadership Killer:
Reclaiming Humility in an Age of Arrogance* (Little Leaps Press, 2018), 88.
"described 'as the finest warrior…'" R. Sisk, "Gates Wanted McChrystal to
Fight for His Job," Military.com, February 3, 2014, military.com/daily-
news/2014/02/03/gates-wanted-mcchrystal-to-fight-for-his-job.html.
"'You're not personally deserving…'" S. McChrystal, interview with author, 2019.
"humble leaders understand that…" Ou et al., "Connections to Top
Management."
"demonstrates a phenomenon that…" S. Sloman, *The Knowledge Illusion: Why
We Never Think Alone* (Riverhead Books, 2017); L. Rozenblit and F. Keil,
"The Misunderstood Limits of Folk Science," *Trends in Cognitive Sciences*
26, no. 5 (2002): 521–62, ncbi.nlm.nih.gov/pmc/articles/PMC3062901.
"we know embarrassingly little…" Harari, *21 Lessons*.
"'The chief task in life is simply…'" Epictetus, *Discourses*, 2.5.4–5, quoted
in R. Holiday, "Control and Choice," Daily Stoic, dailystoic.com/
control-and-choice.
"his circles of control and concern…" Covey, *7 Habits*.
"'the longer you're there…'" J. Sink, "Obama: 'Irony of the Presidential Office'
Is the Humility It Teaches," The Hill, January 21, 2013, video, thehill.
com/video/administration/278349-obama-irony-of-the-presidential-
office-is-humility-.
"Your power consists…" S. Sinek, *The Infinite Game* (Portfolio, 2019).

Index

About the Author

AMER KAISSI is an award-winning professor of health care administration at Trinity University, a Top-15 program. He is the author of the book *Intangibles: The Unexpected Traits of High-Performing Healthcare Leaders*, which won the 2019 American College of Healthcare Executives (ACHE) Book of the Year Award. At Trinity, Kaissi teaches courses in leadership, professional development, and public speaking and is the director of the Executive Program. Kaissi is a national speaker with Huron/Studer Group and a faculty member with ACHE, the University of Colorado Denver, and Boston College. He is also a certified executive and physician coach. He works with MEDI—a division of Navvis—and with the Leadership Development (TLD) Group as an executive coach, and he consults with hospitals and other organizations in their strategic planning efforts. Kaissi is an avid soccer fan and lives in San Antonio, Texas, with his wife and two teenagers.

Made in the USA
Middletown, DE
02 April 2024